GW01260277

A LITTLE BOOK OF

FOOTBALL

ALLSORTED.

This edition first published in Great Britain in 2024
by Allsorted Ltd, WD19 4BG, U.K.

The facts and statistics in this book are correct up to the end of the 2023/24 season. The data comes from publicly available sources and is presented as correct as far as our knowledge allows. The opinions in this book are personal and individual and are not affiliated to the football club in any way. Any views or opinions represented in this book are personal and belong solely to the book author and do not represent those of people, institutions or organisations that the football club or publisher may or may not be associated with in professional or personal capacity, unless explicitly stated. Any views or opinions are not intended to malign any religious, ethnic group, club, organisation, company or individual.

All rights reserved. No part of this work may be reproduced in any form or by any means, electronic or mechanical, including photocopying, recording or by any information storage and retrieval system, without the prior written permission of the publisher.

© Susanna Geoghegan Gift Publishing
Author: Magnus Allan
Cover design: Milestone Creative
Contents design: Bag of Badgers Ltd
Illustrations: Ludovic Sallé

ISBN: 978-1-915902-60-3

Printed in China

CONTENTS

Introduction	5
Andy Goram	10
Premier League's top scorers	12
The three famous lions of England	14
Gordon Banks	18
Premier League's top scorers per season	22
Peter Schmeichel	24
Top scorers per English top-flight season	28
Roy Keane	30
Women's football	32
Lucy Bronze	38
Crossbars	40
John Terry	44
Premier League goalkeeping clean sheets	46
Virgil Van Dijk	48
Premier League top three positions end-of-season points	50
Football boots	52
Rio Ferdinand	58
The rampant lions of Scotland	60
England caps chart	64
Bobby Moore	66
England clean sheets	70
Sir Stanley Matthews	72
The first FIFA World Cup	76
Gareth Bale	80
Goal nets	83
England goal scorers	86
David Beckham	88
The battle at the bottom	92
Relegated to history	95
Kenny Dalglish	98
Corner flags	101
Value at risk: football and the VAR debate	103
Alan Shearer	108
Dugouts	111
A brief history of balls	114
Home Nations football	120
Republic of Ireland	123
World Cup golden boot winners and goals	122
The record-breaking 2006/07 season	124
Floodlights	128
Thierry Henry	132
Three points for a win	137
The most notorious draw ...	139
Harry Kane	142
Shirt numbers	147
Why the game is always evolving	150
George Best	152
Wild GOAT chase	156

• A LITTLE BOOK OF FOOTBALL •

"I wouldn't say I was the best manager in the business. But I was in the top one."

The greatest manager that England never had, Brian Clough. Just because.

⋆ INTRODUCTION ⋆

English romantic painters gave us an idealised pastoral view of history, showing fair England to be forever bathed in a gentle, dappled light and where everything in this green and pleasant land sparkled in the soft hues of an eternal spring morn. 'Twas a place where honest, rustic fellows in straw hats chewed stalks of hay and leaned against ramshackle – but still worthy – gates, looking like they would happily share their ploughman's lunch with you if you did but ask. Verily.

Like the modern world, on a good day some of what was presented in 18th-century oil paintings might well have been true, but it's interesting to note that English romantic painters rarely risked turning their hands, or indeed brushes, to the theoretically friendly rivalries of inter-village mob football.

There's a simple reason for this. In many cases, the rivalries appear to have been very far from friendly. The game was brutal. Virtually anything went. It was often played between villages on holy days, and seems to have been an opportunity to settle scores. Parish records contain reports of broken limbs, injuries caused by gouging and all manner of unpleasantness. From the sounds of things, everyone playing was exuberantly lubricated with copious amounts of beer, cider, mead and anything else that came to hand. There are records of a game in Northumberland in 1280 where a player died after accidentally running onto another player's dagger ...

It's of little surprise, then, that there were several efforts to get the sport banned, with Edwards II, III and IV, Richard II and Henrys IV and V having a go. Under James I of Scotland, the Football Act of 1424 proclaimed that 'na man play at the fut-ball'. These bans were never that effective, though, and games carried on as soon as no one was looking.

Thoroughly modern footy

While it may have started out as a chaotic village sport, urbanisation and the Industrial Revolution meant that rules started to be put in place. By the mid-19th century, formal football clubs were starting to spring up, with teams within the club playing each other using rules that each club defined.

Before long, these clubs started to play each other – sometimes agreeing a set of rules that they were going to follow during a match; sometimes agreeing to use one set of rules for the first half and another set of rules for the second. While this was a good compromise in the short term, in the longer term no one really wanted to be faffing about before the match playing rock, paper, scissors about whether they were going to play according to the Eton rules or the Cambridge rules. They wanted to get on with the game.

The first national standard set of rules was achieved in 1863. The game was still a long way from where we are today, but it gave players and managers something to work with, something they could take out across the world. You might not speak the same language, but turn up with a football virtually anywhere in the world by the late 19th century, and you'd pretty quickly be able to put a game together – and usually be playing to the same rules.

As each country embraced the sport, they brought their local nuances to the way it was played, often based on local sports that had evolved in parallel or, in some cases, significantly earlier, such as the evasively named Meso-American ball game in South America or *harpastum* in the Roman Empire. On the one hand, this was wonderful; on the other, it's part of the reason why British teams are often outclassed at international competitions. Britain gave football to the world, and the world has kept returning to the back of our nets at speed.

With the mid-point of the 21st century in sight, football's popularity shows no sign of dimming. We are all still arguing about what the best rules are and how they should be applied, but the sport's still growing.

It's come a long way from its allegedly idyllic pastoral roots.

> The oldest surviving football can be seen in Stirling Castle. It's thought to hail from Scotland in about 1540 and was an inflated pig's bladder.

· A LITTLE BOOK OF FOOTBALL ·

"Aim for the sky and you'll reach the ceiling. Aim for the ceiling and you'll stay on the floor."

Bill Shankly simultaneously explains why he was so inspirational as a manager, but less remembered as a player (1,307 goals in all competitions over 783 matches as Liverpool manager, 297 appearances as a right-half for Preston North End ... it's not a perfect comparison, but you didn't pay much for the book).

· A LITTLE BOOK OF FOOTBALL ·

★ ANDY GORAM ★

Andy Goram was simply 'The Goalie', the man who stood between the sticks as Rangers won the Scottish Premier Division in 1991/92, 1992/93, 1994/95, 1995/96 and 1996/97, the Scottish Cup in 1991/92, 1992/93 and 1995/96 and the Scottish League Cup in 1992/93 and 1996/97. He also won the Scottish Challenge Cup with Queen of the South in 2002/03.

He spent the early 1980s at Oldham before moving north of the border to join Hibernian, where his father had also briefly been a goalie. He spent four years at Hibs before heading westward to join Rangers, where he spent seven years at the heart of the defence of one of Rangers' most fondly remembered teams.

English by birth, Goram was called up for an England under-21 match, but because he was unused, caretaker manager Alex Ferguson offered him a place in the Scotland team in 1985 as a result of his father being Edinburgh-born. He made 43 appearances for Scotland over the next 13 years. A second phone call from Ferguson later in his career led to Goram enjoying a brief loan spell with Manchester United in 2000/01, adding an English Premier League medal to his career haul.

In his spare time, he was also an international cricketer, turning out for Scotland. Astonishingly, he tended to don the gloves as a wicket keeper.

· A LITTLE BOOK OF FOOTBALL ·

Player	Club
Mohamed Salah	Chelsea, Liverpool
Robbie Fowler	Liverpool, Leeds United, Manchester City, Cardiff City, Blackburn Rovers
Jermain Defoe	West Ham United, Tottenham Hotspur, Portsmouth, Sunderland, AFC Bournemouth, Rangers
Thierry Henry	Arsenal
Frank Lampard	West Ham, Chelsea, Manchester City
Sergio Agüero	Manchester City
Andrew Cole	Arsenal, Bristol City, Newcastle United, Manchester United, Blackburn Rovers, Fulham, Manchester City, Portsmouth, Sunderland, Nottingham Forest
Wayne Rooney	Everton, Manchester United, Derby County
Harry Kane	Tottenham Hotspur
Alan Shearer	Southampton, Blackburn Rovers, Newcastle United

Goals

· A LITTLE BOOK OF FOOTBALL ·

★ PREMIER LEAGUE'S TOP SCORERS ★

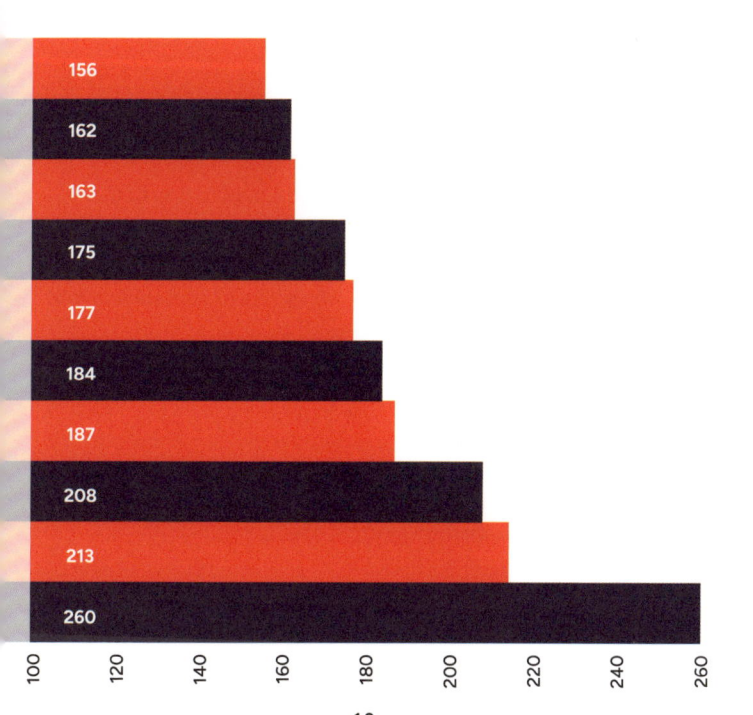

Goals
156
162
163
175
177
184
187
208
213
260

★ THE THREE FAMOUS ★ LIONS OF ENGLAND

The last lions to have lived on the British Isles are estimated to have died out around 12,000–14,000 years ago (Tuesday, 4 October 10,873 BC at around 11:56 pm, to be more specific). The fossil records suggest that they were impressive beasties, around 25% larger than the lions that currently mooch majestically across the Serengeti. Given that they've been gone for a long time, why do they adorn the shirts of several English sports teams, including the national football teams?

The answer is not all that deep.

Back in the day, Roman legionaries liked to have special logos on the standards that they carried into battle. This helped different parts of an army recognise one another so they could go about their business of invading and plundering with a modicum of organisation. The standards tended to show badass animals, such as eagles, lions and bears — rather than innocuous animals like donkeys, hedgehogs and butterflies — because it was a rufty-tufty world of swords, sandals and togas.

The tradition continued and became more formalised as time went on, with noble families having to consult books of heraldry as they came up with their coats of arms, and then having to consult them again as families (inter)married. These coats of arms were adapted to give people an instant idea about who was the most important person in the room at any one time.

King Henry I, fourth son of William the Conqueror, ascended to the throne of England in 1100 AD. His coat of arms was a single lion. His second wife, Adeliza of Louvain, also had a lion on her coat of arms and so, when he married her, Henry updated his status with a second lion.

Time went by, kings rose and kings fell ... In 1152, Henry of Anjou (who became Henry II in 1154), married Eleanor of Aquitaine. She also had a lion on her family crest. Under their son, Richard the Lionheart, the two lions became three. At which point, the royal families thought that they were putting too much work in the direction of the very expensive executive heraldic experts and have stuck to the three lions ever since.

When international football started to become a thing and the English and Scottish men's teams faced each other for the first time 720 years later, the English team put this pride of lions on their shirts, and there they have stayed. The only change to the crest came in 1949 when the crown on top was removed, presumably so that the football team's shirts didn't get mixed up with the cricket team's shirts when they went into the wash. Or something. Incidentally, two years earlier, in 1947, England moved to the iconic red away shirts. Prior to this the second kit had been blue.

Speaking of cricket, the English football team's first-choice white shirt stems from that first international against Scotland in 1872. The Scotland team were playing in navy and the story goes that the white shirts England played in were actually cricket shirts because that's all that the English Football Association (FA) could lay their hands on. It's hard to confirm the truth or otherwise of this rumour.

• A LITTLE BOOK OF FOOTBALL •

> **"Rugby is a game for barbarians played by gentlemen. Football is a game for gentlemen played by barbarians."**

Celebrated wit Oscar Wilde didn't play the beautiful game, but was not a bad boxer in his day.

· A LITTLE BOOK OF FOOTBALL ·

★ GORDON BANKS ★

• A LITTLE BOOK OF FOOTBALL •

Sheffield-born Gordon Banks is responsible for what has been widely described as the 'Greatest Save Ever Made'. This is a big statement until you realise that it was made against a downward header at the left post from Pelé at almost point-blank range after Jairzinho ran down the right wing, broke through the defence and delivered a superbly placed cross. The reactions and the strength that the save took were exceptional, and Pelé himself regularly stated that he couldn't understand how Banks stopped his shot.

The fact that Banks suffered food poisoning and was unable to play in the next match is often cited as one of the key reasons why England were knocked out of the 1970 World Cup in the next match.

His skills and reactions were presumably a mixture of innate ability and extensive training, but Banks's strength was built up in his teenage years when he worked as a coal bagger (putting coal into bags and then lugging the bags to where they needed to be) and a hod carrier (putting bricks on to carts and then lugging the carts to where they needed to be). There was a lot of moving stuff around back in them days.

He joined Chesterfield's youth set-up in 1953, turning professional at 21 in 1958. He moved on to Leicester after only 23 professional matches with Chesterfield, staying with the Foxes for eight years and making 293 appearances. His claim on the number one spot was threatened by rising star Peter Shilton and he moved on to Stoke City, where he stayed for six years (with a smattering of loan spells along the way), before rounding out his career with a bit of time playing in the North American Soccer League.

His nephew is the drummer with legendary Sheffield band Pulp. History does not record whether he or Jarvis Cocker ever worked as hod carriers.

• A LITTLE BOOK OF FOOTBALL •

> "Every kid around the world who plays soccer wants to be Pelé. I have a great responsibility to show them not just how to be like a soccer player, but how to be like a man."

Pelé, who needs neither introduction nor surname, explains that with great power comes great responsibility.

·A LITTLE BOOK OF FOOTBALL·

Season	Player	Goals
2004/05	Thierry Henry (Arsenal)	25
2005/06	Thierry Henry (Arsenal)	27
2006/07	Didier Drogba (Chelsea)	20
2007/08	Cristiano Ronaldo (Manchester United)	31
2008/09	Nicolas Anelka (Chelsea)	19
2009/10	Didier Drogba (Chelsea)	29
2010/11	Dimitar Berbatov (Manchester United), Carlos Tevez (Manchester City)	20
2011/12	Robin van Persie (Arsenal)	30
2012/13	Robin van Persie (Manchester United)	26
2013/14	Luis Suárez (Liverpool)	31
2014/15	Sergio Agüero (Manchester City)	26
2015/16	Harry Kane (Tottenham Hotspur)	25
2016/17	Harry Kane (Tottenham Hotspur)	29
2017/18	Mohamed Salah (Liverpool)	32
2018/19	Mohamed Salah (Liverpool), Sadio Mané (Liverpool), Pierre-Emerick Aubameyang (Arsenal)	22
2019/20	Jamie Vardy (Leicester City)	23
2020/21	Harry Kane (Tottenham Hotspur)	23
2021/22	Mohamed Salah (Liverpool), Son Heung-min (Tottenham Hotspur)	23
2022/23	Erling Haaland (Manchester City)	36
2023/24	Erling Haaland (Manchester City)	27

· A LITTLE BOOK OF FOOTBALL ·

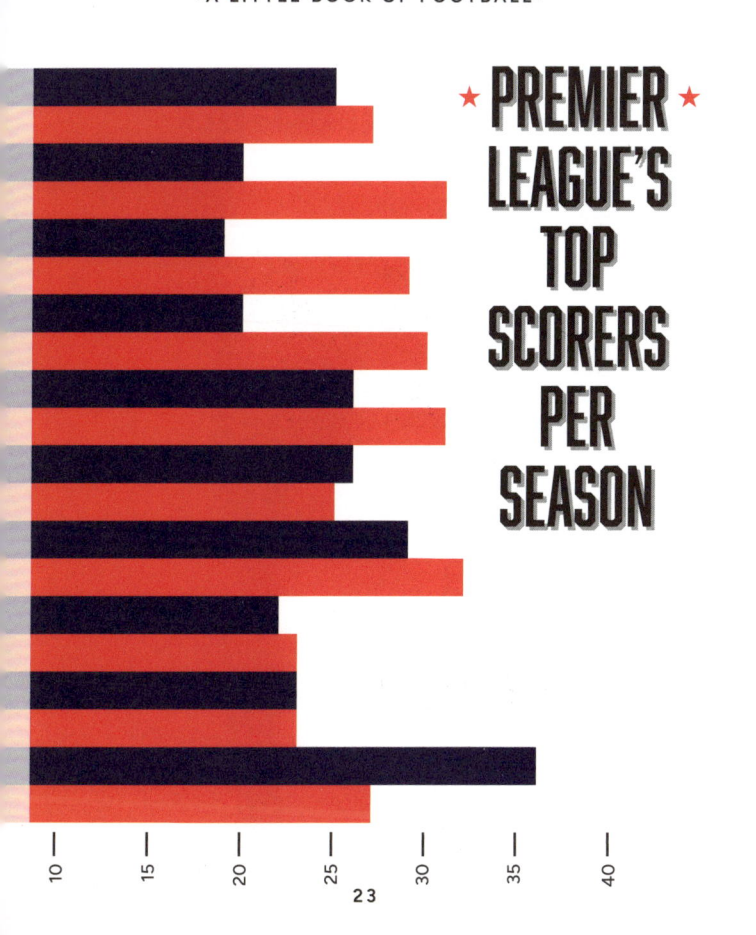

★ PREMIER ★
LEAGUE'S
TOP
SCORERS
PER
SEASON

·A LITTLE BOOK OF FOOTBALL·

★ PETER SCHMEICHEL ★

Peter Schmeichel stood at the heart of one of the most successful football teams that the world has ever seen: the Manchester United team that rose at the start of the Premier League era and dominated English and European football for a decade.

He also played a vital role in helping Denmark to win the 1992 European Cup, despite the fact that his national team only qualified after the implosion of Yugoslavia a few weeks before the tournament started. And before anyone starts moaning about the Danes having an easy route, it's worth pointing out that the team drew with England and beat France, only shipping a single goal in the group stage, overcame the Netherlands (on penalties) in the semis, and then beat a newly reunified Germany by two goals and a clean sheet in the final.

From a league perspective, Schmeichel joined Man U for a modest £505,000 from Danish side Brøndby IF, who he had helped reach the semi-final of the 1990/91 UEFA Cup (denied a place in the final by an 88th-minute strike by Roma's Rudi Völler).

As you would expect from a goalkeeper, Schmeichel was not prolific at the other end of the pitch, scoring only once for Manchester United in the UEFA Cup against Roto Volograd in 1995. Six years later, he became the first goalie to score in the

Premier League, finding the net for Aston Villa against Everton. It was coolly taken and warmly applauded by even the Toffees fans.

Ultimately, though, it was his prowess as a shot stopper that makes him a legend – he was a key component in a team that won the Premier League in 1992/93, 1993/94, 1995/96, 1996/97 and 1998/99, the FA Cup in 1993/94, 1995/96 and 1998/99, the Football League Cup in 1991/92, the FA Charity Shield in 1993, 1994, 1996 and 1997, the UEFA Champions League in 1998/99 and the European Super Cup in 1991.

Those are memories that keep United fans warm to this very day.

While the rest of us tried to keep up with Joe Wicks or made terrible banana bread, Schmeichel formed a band during the Covid-19 lockdown and has recently indulged in some light touring around Denmark's most iconic rock n'roll venues. It's a reminder of quite how much time football players have on their hands after their playing careers come to a close.

• A LITTLE BOOK OF FOOTBALL •

"Football is the only thing that can bring together an entire country, regardless of political or religious differences."

Zinedine Zidane, a player, a philosopher, a man who really who knew how to use his head.

·A LITTLE BOOK OF FOOTBALL·

Player	Year	Goals
Jimmy Greaves (Tottenham Hotspur)	1963/64	35
Tommy Lawton (Everton)	1938/39	35
Jack Bowers (Derby County)	1932/33	35
Bobby Parker (Everton)	1914/15	35
Erling Haaland (Manchester City)	2022/23	36
Bobby Smith (Tottenham Hotspur)	1957/58	36
Ron Davies (Southampton)	1966/67	37
Jimmy Greaves (Tottenham Hotspur)	1962/63	37
Dennis Westcott (Wolverhampton Wanderers)	1946/47	37
Jimmy Trotter (Sheffield Wednesday)	1926/27	37
Fred Morris (West Bromwich Albion)	1919/20	37
John Charles (Leeds United)	1956/57	38
Joe Smith (Bolton Wanderers)	1920/21	38
Bert Freeman (Everton)	1908/09	38
W.G. Richardson (West Bromwich Albion)	1935/36	39
Jimmy Greaves (Chelsea)	1960/61	41
Vic Watson (West Ham United)	1929/30	41
Ted Drake (Arsenal)	1934/35	42
Dave Halliday (Sunderland)	1928/29	43
Ted Harper (Blackburn Rovers)	1925/26	43
Dixie Dean (Everton)	1931/32	44
Tom Waring (Aston Villa)	1930/31	49
Dixie Dean (Everton)	1927/28	60

·A LITTLE BOOK OF FOOTBALL·

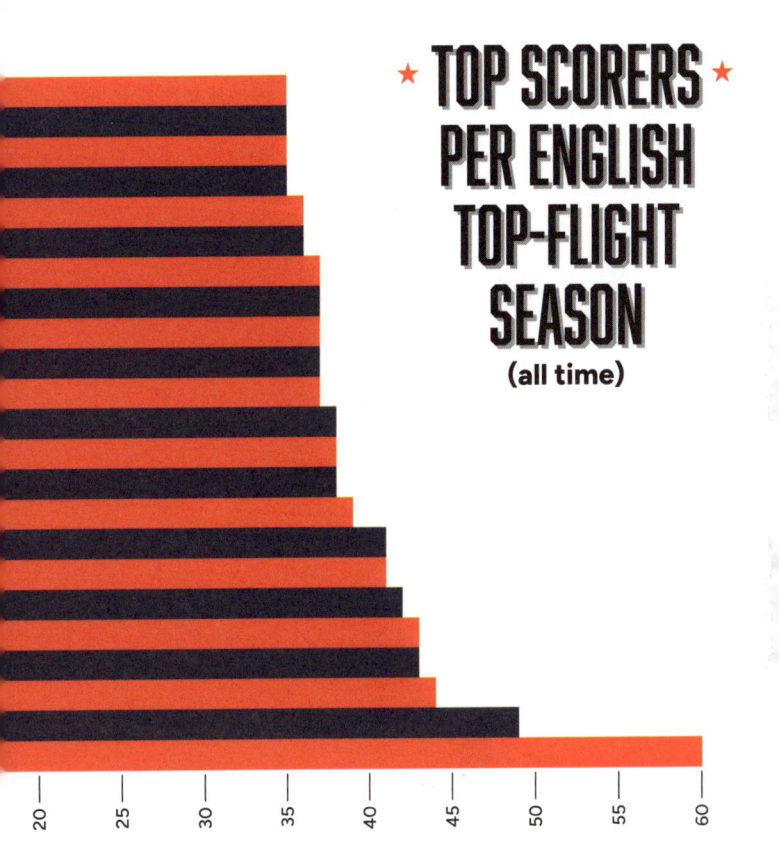

★ TOP SCORERS ★ PER ENGLISH TOP-FLIGHT SEASON
(all time)

• A LITTLE BOOK OF FOOTBALL •

★ ROY KEANE ★

The thing about a team sport like football is that you need a mix of personalities in the dressing room if you are going to get things done. Roy Keane certainly ticked a lot of boxes on the personality front, appearing to exist on the extreme end of irascibility at all times. He never let his playing standards slip and he expected the same of everyone on his team. No nonsense, no excuses.

He was initially passed over for an apprenticeship before catching the eye of Brian Clough, a man who defined no-nonsense management throughout the 1970s and 1980s. Clough took him to Nottingham Forest in 1990, where he stayed for three years, made 114 appearances and scored 26 goals.

From there he joined Manchester United as they ran rampant across the first decade and a half of the Premier League. He made 326 league appearances for Sir Alex Ferguson's high-performance team, finding the net 33 times and basically giving the team an armour-plated backbone and the ability to breath fire. There are utterly unfounded suggestions that the Red Devil turned to Keane when it wanted its trident sharpening, and that the Irishman did it with but a glance.

Keane made 67 appearances for the Republic or Ireland, scoring nine times.

★ WOMEN'S FOOTBALL ★

It appears that women were getting their skirts dirty and indulging in football even before the game started to become what it is today. In 1580, for example, Sir Philip Sidney – poet, courtier, scholar, soldier and general chap about town – published a poem that included the lines:

> A tyme there is for all, my mother often sayes,
> When she, with skirts tuckt very hy, with girles at football playes.

Which roughly translates to: My mother says that there is a time for us all, and when it was her time, she tucked in her skirts (very high), and played football with the girls.

It's not exactly till receipts, match-day programmes or sepia photographs of the terraces, but it does suggest that there was some acceptance of women playing football back in the Elizabethan era, particularly given Sidney's position in high society at the time.

The new dawn

Looking at what you might call the organised era of football over the last 150 years, women's football in Britain has been allowed to enjoy around a century of history. There have basically been four distinct phases: the new dawn; the darkest night; the new-new dawn; and what we have today.

At the dawn of football, some women looked at the emerging game, thought to themselves, *we can do that*, and then got on with it. The earliest recorded women's football games were held in the 1880s and attracted healthy crowds. It's interesting to note that the first international football matches between England and Scotland were actually a series of women's games that attracted around 5,000 supporters. However, it should be noted that two matches in the proposed three-match series were abandoned due to rioting and pitch invasions.

The men's game at the time was still struggling with the concept of professionalism, but the women's game was developed and promoted by local businesspeople (yeah, all right, businessmen) who were looking for ways to bring crowds to their stadiums and make their tills sing.

Women's football continued for the next couple of decades, often attracting good crowds and certainly generating debate, but the various attempts to form a league didn't really take off. With the outbreak of war in 1914 and with many men going off to fight, women's matches, often held in support of charity, began to enjoy renewed support. This continued once hostilities came to an end, although there was still opposition to the sport from several elements in society.

The darkest night

Women's football continued to grow even after the war, but so did the opposition to it. This led to the second phase – the darkest night – in 1921, when women's football was to all intents and purposes banned for the next 50 years. It's worth noting two things here.

Firstly, the FA has apologised and everyone involved in the ban, which was lifted in 1971, has subsequently moved on from their positions within the organisation.

Secondly, the FA did not technically ban women's football. They simply said that women's teams could not use FA-supported facilities or equipment. Which simply had the unintended consequence of making it impossible to set up and manage a football team.

There are a lot of things about the ban that make you raise an eyebrow in the direction of our forebears. One of these is the way that it was instituted. The English FA had a lot of power around the world at the time, so several other associations followed its lead as soon as it instituted the ban. The thing that rankles is that the Dick, Kerr Ladies, one of the most famous English women's teams of the day, had already left for a tour of Canada and the United States (US) in 1922 when the Canadian FA followed suit and put its own ban in place. The team had to hastily set up games against men's teams in the US to pay for their tickets home. This they did, playing nine games, which ended with three wins, three draws and three losses. This possibly makes a point about equality all on its own.

The new-new dawn

Despite the hurdles that were put in its way, women's football did not go away. Games were put on at various points throughout the next 50 years, and by the early 1970s the FA decided – well, were forced – to rescind its ban. This new-new dawn, it should be noted, was a long way from actively supporting the game, but it was at least a step in the right direction.

What we have today

By the 1990s there were tentative attempts to bring the women's game together around the world for a somewhat tentatively titled World Championship, but media companies were supportive, fan bases kept growing and momentum has been growing ever since. 80,000 people flocked to Wembley in 2019 to watch the Lionesses take on Germany in a friendly and FA Cup finals now regularly attract 40,000 spectators.

• A LITTLE BOOK OF FOOTBALL •

> "I don't call myself a women's footballer; I say I'm a footballer."

Lucy Bronze makes a simple but important point.

• A LITTLE BOOK OF FOOTBALL •

★ LUCY BRONZE ★

Full-back Lucy Bronze has won the Champions League five times. She's won the Women's Super League three times. She's won the FA WSL Cup and the Women's FA Cup twice. She's won the European Cup with England as well as UEFA Women's Under-19 Championship.

She's also won the Division 1 Féminine in France three times, the Coupe de France feminine twice and the Trophée des Championnes once. And you can also add two Liga F victories (the top women's league in Spain), as well as the Supercopa de España Femenina twice and the Copa de la Reina.

Her career has so far taken her from Sunderland to Everton, across the park to Liverpool, down the road to Manchester City, over the water to Lyon, back to Manchester City and then back over the water to Barcelona.

Basically, she goes places and she wins stuff because she's an exceptional footballer.

★ CROSSBARS ★

The first rules of football stated that goals needed to be marked out by goalposts, but this led to arguments when some players started claiming goals where the ball might indeed have gone between the sticks but was clearly destined for Row Z (not that football grounds in the 1860s tended to have lettered rows, or indeed stadiums, but hopefully you take the point). In response, a simple tape was required to be stretched out between the goalposts from 1866. This led to arguments because the tape moved in the wind. So, to stop all the arguing that inevitably followed, in 1882, solid crossbars were mandated, in theory doing away with all the arguments.

In practice, astonishingly, there were still arguments.

To pick an example at random: 1966. Now, you may not have ever heard any England football fans talking about this, but 1966 was the first, and so far only, time that the Three Lions have won the FIFA World Cup.

It happened like this: Deep in extra time, Alan Ball offered a superbly weighted cross into the German box which was pounced on by Geoff Hurst who poked the ball in the direction of the net ... it beat the keeper and bounced down off the crossbar and probably over the goal line before bouncing back out again. England celebrated the goal, and the referee, after consulting with the linesman agreed (allegedly using sign language because they didn't speak a common language).

Many folk (and to be fair, by many folk, we mostly mean Germans, so perhaps many *volk* is more appropriate) are still arguing about whether Geoff Hurst's extra-time goal, which took the score to 3–2 in England's favour, should have stood because they are not convinced that the whole of the ball had made it over the line.

Fifty years on and the debate is still generating headlines, with various academics, pundits and emerging technology experts voicing their opinions, secure in the knowledge that it won't make a blind bit of difference. Because if you are going to open the can of worms that is the third English goal, you should also ask if the Germans should have been given the free kick that led to their second goal equaliser and took the game into extra time in the first place …

No one's come up with anything better than the crossbar, but it didn't stop arguments until goal-line technology was finally included in the 2013/14 season.

What can we make of this? Tape is better than nothing and a crossbar is better than tape, but contentious decisions will always be part of the game.

> **The third England goal in the 1966 World Cup definitely did cross the line, by the way.**
>
> In 2016, Sky Sports pundit Jamie Carragher and presenter Ed Chamberlain used EA Sports performance software to put the nearly 60-year debate to bed once and for all.

• A LITTLE BOOK OF FOOTBALL •

"Football is a game you play with your brains."

Johan Cruyff, famous for his turns, delivers a twist.

·A LITTLE BOOK OF FOOTBALL·

★ JOHN TERRY ★

John Terry has been an active supporter of women's football and was also an astonishingly good football player, holding the line for the Chelsea team that dominated English football in the noughties. He was initially part of the West Ham youth team, before being enticed to west London, aged 14, in 1995 — where he stayed until the end of the Premier League 2016/17 season.

Terry was good with both feet and read the game exceptionally well, which made him an excellent central defender and an active participant in Chelsea's frequent forays further up the field. In 492 Premier League appearances, he knocked in 41 goals (17 with his head) and delivered 12 assists, but most importantly for a defender, he helped Chelsea enjoy 214 Premier League clean sheets, which translates to a little under 45% of his time at the top level.

He also enjoyed a 10-year spell at the heart of the England side, making 78 appearances, 34 of them as captain.

·A LITTLE BOOK OF FOOTBALL·

Keeper

Paul Robinson (Leeds United, Tottenham Hotspur, Blackburn Rovers, Burnley)

Lukasz Fabianski (Arsenal, Swansea City, West Ham United)

Ben Foster (Man United, Birmingham City, West Bromwich Albion, Watford)

Thomas Sørensen (Aston Villa, Sunderland, Stoke City)

Jussi Jääskeläinen (Bolton Wanderers, West Ham United)

Ederson (Manchester City)

Shay Given (Newcastle United, Man City, Aston Villa, Blackburn Rovers, Stoke City)

Hugo Lloris (Tottenham Hotspur)

Joe Hart (Manchester City, Birmingham City, West Ham United, Burnley)

Peter Schmeichel (Manchester United, Manchester City, Aston Villa)

Brad Friedel (Blackburn Rovers, Aston Villa, Tottenham Hotspur, Liverpool)

Tim Howard (Everton, Manchester United)

Edwin van der Sar (Manchester United, Fulham)

Pepe Reina (Liverpool, Aston Villa)

Nigel Martyn (Leeds United, Everton, Crystal Palace)

David Seaman (Arsenal, Manchester City)

David de Gea (Manchester United)

Mark Schwarzer (Middlesbrough, Fulham, Chelsea, Leicester City)

David James (Liverpool, Portsmouth, Aston Villa, Man City, West Ham United)

Petr Čech (Chelsea, Arsenal)

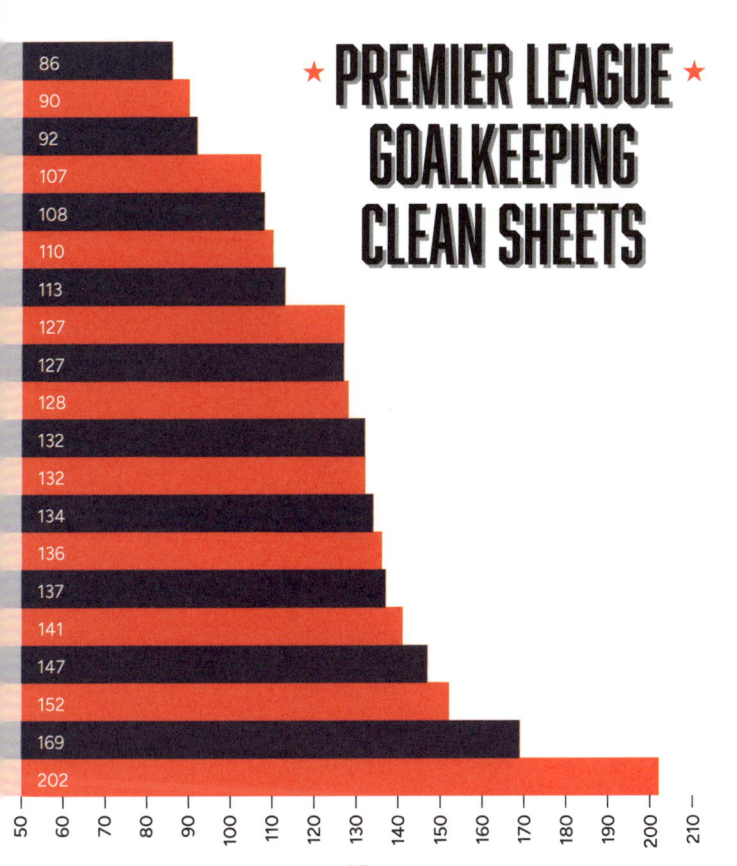

★ PREMIER LEAGUE GOALKEEPING CLEAN SHEETS ★

Clean Sheets
86
90
92
107
108
110
113
127
127
128
132
132
134
136
137
141
147
152
169
202

·A LITTLE BOOK OF FOOTBALL·

★ VIRGIL VAN DIJK ★

Virgil van Dijk has made 258 appearances in the Premier League, coming away with 101 clean sheets for Liverpool and Southampton. He played 38 times in Liverpool's title-winning season in 2019/20, only conceding 33 goals and scoring five — all of them with his head, because he's a 6 foot 5 central defender. This means he can jump for crosses and corners that are well out of the reach of most people.

He spent his first couple of years as a professional at Groningen, in the Netherlands, before joining Celtic, where he won the Scottish Premiership twice, as well as the Scottish League Cup. From there he went to Southampton for two-and-a-bit seasons, and then headed up to Liverpool — where he has enjoyed seven glittering seasons so far.

Van Dijk has immense confidence with the ball, an ability to read the game and is known to be able to wallop a free kick with precision when needed. Despite his height, he's also very agile, which is a very handy attribute when timing a tackle.

He joined the Netherlands national team in 2015 and has played with them 74 times so far. He has been captain since 2018.

· A LITTLE BOOK OF FOOTBALL ·

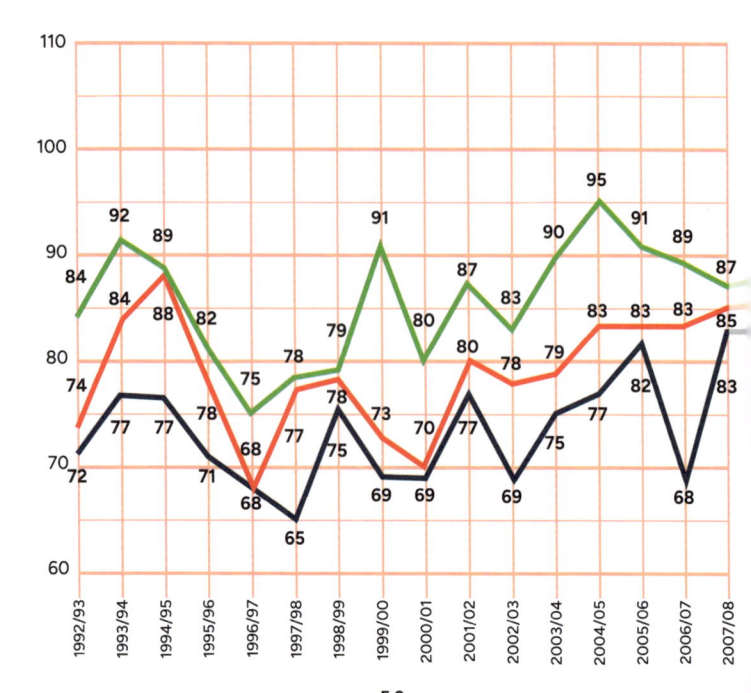

Winners / Second / Third

Season	Winners	Second	Third
1992/93	84	74	72
1993/94	92	84	77
1994/95	89	88	77
1995/96	82	78	71
1996/97	75	68	68
1997/98	78	77	65
1998/99	79	78	75
1999/00	91	73	69
2000/01	80	70	69
2001/02	87	80	77
2002/03	83	78	69
2003/04	90	79	75
2004/05	95	83	77
2005/06	91	83	82
2006/07	89	83	68
2007/08	87	85	83

·A LITTLE BOOK OF FOOTBALL·

★ PREMIER LEAGUE TOP THREE ★ POSITIONS END-OF-SEASON POINTS

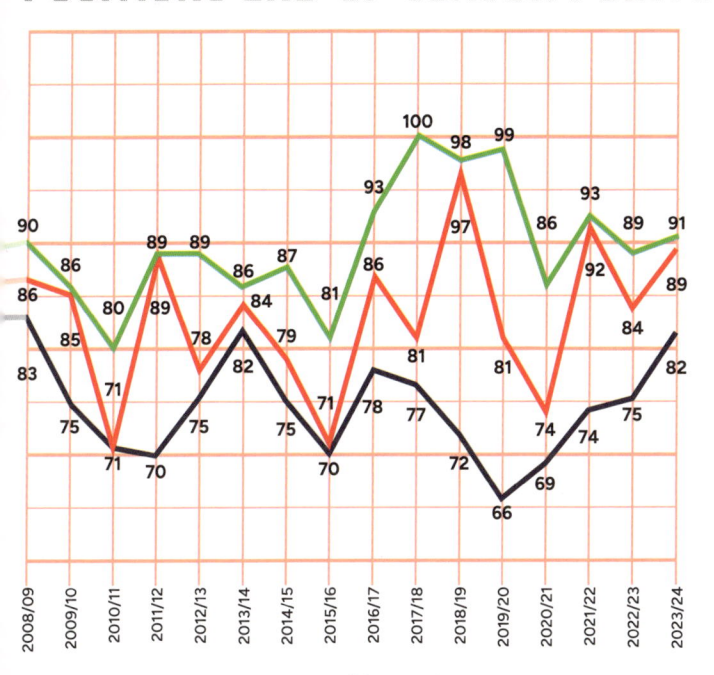

Season	1st (green)	2nd (orange)	3rd (black)
2008/09	90	86	83
2009/10	86	85	75
2010/11	80	71	71
2011/12	89	89	70
2012/13	89	78	75
2013/14	86	84	82
2014/15	87	79	75
2015/16	81	71	70
2016/17	93	86	78
2017/18	100	81	77
2018/19	98	97	72
2019/20	99	81	66
2020/21	86	74	69
2021/22	93	92	74
2022/23	89	84	75
2023/24	91	89	82

★ FOOTBALL BOOTS ★

What did he use for a ball?

It's possible that King Henry VIII was the greatest innovator that the world has ever seen. He revolutionised virtually every aspect of British society during his reign (1509–1547), setting the country on its course for the modern age. Historians can have as much fun as they like debating the rights and wrongs of that, but they will struggle to deny this absolute fact: he owned the first recorded pair of boots made specifically for football.

This is, of course, different from owning the first pair of boots made specifically for football. Football was a popular and frequently banned pastime (see page 6), so the chances are that other people owned boots that were specially adapted for the brutality of the then-modern game. The difference is that Henry VIII was a monarch: monarchs have courtiers who hang on to their every bit of paper; those bits of paper are stalked by historians; and those historians have discovered a record of the purchase of a pair of specially designed football boots among the 17,000 items of clothing owned by the king.

We don't actually have the boots, but we know that they existed. They were made of Spanish leather, cost four shillings and were made by Good King Henry's royal cordwainer – the sumptuously named Cornelius Johnson, who sounds like he played for Northampton Town in the 1970s.

What we don't know is whether His Royal Highness Henry VIII paid the extra 14 florins to have HVIIIR emblazoned regally across them, or whether his football boots would have had the more artful HR8 stitched tastefully down the side.

How did legs keep getting broken?

When football started to move from the fields and villages to the pitches and towns, people tended to simply play in the boots that they had for work. In the case of the working classes, this tended to mean thick leather, limited grip on the mud and, quite often, steel toecaps. Which may go some way to explain the broken legs that footballers frequently suffered.

The original 13 rules of football included the stipulation that: 'No player shall wear projecting nails, iron plates or gutta-percha on the soles or heels of his boots'. Gutta-percha is a natural rubber that could be used to make their boots harder, but it's the prohibition of projecting nails that really catches the eye. It's probable that they were being used as a form of rudimentary stud, but there are other ways they could presumably have been used. Football was a tough game back in the day.

Actual studs were introduced in the mid-1880s, but it wasn't until the 1950s that boots started to have screw-in studs that enabled players to adapt their boots to different weather conditions.

At this point, though, boots were still predominantly made of heavy leather, which did not offer a lot of subtlety in terms of movement. The growth of football in southern Europe and other, sunnier, climates across the world led to the development of lighter boots that were better suited to the increasingly beautiful game.

Ball to foot

By the early 1960s, you could have football boots in any colour you wanted so long as the colour you wanted was black, but this started to change at the end of the decade. Alan Ball led the charge, exhibiting a pair of snazzy white Hummel boots in the Charity Shield match at the start of the 1970/71 season. This allegedly tripled Hummel's annual orders for their white boots overnight.

It was the start of the season so maybe lots of people needed new boots, but the irony (even more allegedly) is that Hummel didn't have boots in Ball's size, so the pair that he was wearing were actually Ball's Adidas boots painted white and given Hummel branding. We were a long way from HD TVs at this point, so it's a bit hard to go back and check.

Ball's boots were hot on the heels of the iconic Telstar football (see page 116), and as technology improved over the next few years, boots became as vibrant as the balls they kicked. These days, most new boots from major manufacturers are accompanied by gushing press releases and unboxing videos by excitable folk on social media who shamelessly use the word 'colourway' when what they mean is 'colour', 'chassis' when they mean 'upper' and 'definitive forefoot lockdown' when they mean 'step'. This is what they call progress.

It's how you wear it

On the subject of the kids, though, there is concern about the amount of pressure that social media is putting on us all, but in a lot of ways the myriad of quality football boots available is one way that life has become easier. Back in the day, there were usually only a few boots that everyone wanted: Pelé's Puma Kings in 1970, Beckenbauer's Adidas Copa Mundial in 1982, Gascoigne's Predators in 1994.

As a kid, if you had those boots, you were a footballer; if you didn't have those boots, you weren't. If you played for a team at the weekend, you knew who to watch on the pitch because they'd be the ones bringing out that generation's capital B Boots.

The thing is, though, these days there are so many great boots out there, it's impossible to judge what you are up against. A random search at a major British sports retailer shows that there are nearly 150 football boots currently available for £200 or more. This means there's so much less pressure to have the 'right' boots nowadays because there are so many different 'right' boots to choose from.

· A LITTLE BOOK OF FOOTBALL ·

"Football is like chess, only without the dice."

German forward Lukas Podolski offers a masterclass in the perfect quote.

· A LITTLE BOOK OF FOOTBALL ·

★ RIO FERDINAND ★

• A LITTLE BOOK OF FOOTBALL •

Rio Ferdinand comes across as a nice guy with more than a hint of south-east London steel about him. His athletic prowess and physical coordination was apparent from a young age, and he participated and competed in a range of competitions across a spread of sports before being scouted for the West Ham academy (by Frank Lampard Sr, no less) in 1992.

He spent eight years with the Hammers before joining Leeds in 2000. He became club captain at the start of the 2001/02 campaign before signing for Manchester United a year later as the most expensive British footballer and the most expensive defender in the world at the time. Very few would deny that he proved to be worth the investment over the next 12 seasons.

Ferdinand was a key component of the Manchester United team that won the Premier League six times, the Football League Cup twice, the FA Community Shield four times, the FIFA Club World Cup and the UEFA Champions League once each. He was also part of the senior England set-up for the best part of 14 years, claiming 81 caps and taking the captain's armband several times.

Since hanging up his professional football boots, Ferdinand has worked as a pundit on television and used his voice to campaign on a range of social issues.

★ THE RAMPANT LIONS ★ OF SCOTLAND

Scotland has been almost as consistent with the lion rampant on the shirt as England, although for a decade or so from the 1880s they wore a thistle on their chest, a motif usually associated with rugby. By the turn of the 20th century the lion was back in place, and there it has stayed – although these days, with enhanced printing and materials, it is rearing up in a field of thistles. Potentially having stood on one.

They've also stuck mostly with dark blue shirts, known fondly as the 'Navy Blue', although there was a dalliance with a very fetching pink and primrose yellow hooped affair from time to time in the 1880s and 1890s, and again around 1905–1908. The colours were selected in recognition of Archibald Primrose, the fifth Earl of Rosebery (and briefly Prime Minister of the United Kingdom), who was one of the Scottish FA's early patrons. He was also a keen horse racer and his riders raced in the same colours, which are sometimes still echoed these days in Scotland's away strips. Unlike England and the cricket shirts, there is no suggestion that the Scottish football team ever turned out in jockeys' silks.

★ SHIN PADS ★

The shin pad was not invented in Britain. It was not even developed specifically for football. To find the earliest known use of a shin pad, you've got to go back two-and-a-half millennia to ancient Greece, where various forms of protective guards, known then as 'greaves', were used to protect the legs of both athletes and soldiers. However, there's a decent chance that some form of shin protection has been in use since the dawn of humanity because, let's face it, bashing your shin on something is almost as painful as stubbing your toe. Some bright spark will probably have worked something out slightly after the discovery of fire. Maybe earlier, if everyone was stumbling around in the dark bashing their shins on things.

From a football perspective, though, the history of the shin pad is a little murky. The favourite story revolves around Samuel Widdowson, the key man for Nottingham Forest in the 1870s who also happened to be a keen runner, hurdler and cricketer.

Widdowson was well known, and widely feared by defenders, for his dribbling ability, and when you are widely feared by defenders in the 1870s, their primary strategy was to chop you down to size. Two footed.

Broken legs were common, so one day in 1874 Widdowson is said to have taken one of his cricket pads, cut it down to size and strapped it to his leg. He is said to have been widely ridiculed for the idea – and then everyone else came round to his way of thinking and the shin pad was adopted by footballers across the land.

FIFA didn't actually mandate the wearing of shin pads until 1990, but interestingly, the first recorded game where both teams were wearing shin pads was between Newcastle and Woolwich Arsenal in 1894.

The reason that this is interesting is that Woolwich Arsenal was formed in 1886 when a handful of former Nottingham Forest players moved to south London in search of work and formed a football team in their spare time. The Forest players still had their former team kits, and they asked their former club if they could have some more old shirts so they could fit out their new team, which is why the Arsenal home strip is still red and white. It's a bit of a stretch, but it could be that the shin pads that came to be used in the match between the Magpies and the Gunners came directly from the Forest kit room where Widdowson had been inspired two decades before.

But it could also just be coincidence. History can be murky unless there's a monarch involved …

What is fact, though, is that shin pads weren't the only innovation that Widdowson was involved in. He went on to become the first football referee to use a whistle instead of a white flag to signal an infringement, and he is also said to have officiated in the first match to use goal nets, which you'll be glad to hear we talk more about on page 83.

> **FIFA Law 4 states that shin pads should be entirely covered by socks, made of a suitable material and provide a reasonable degree of protection – which is loosely applied by some well-known footballers. There are those that say Jack Grealish uses inexplicably tiny shinpads, but that could just be a question of perspective because that bloke has massive calves.**

· A LITTLE BOOK OF FOOTBALL ·

Player	Club
Harry Kane	Tottenham Hotspu, Bayern Munich
Billy Wright	Wolverhampton Wanderers
Frank Lampard	West Ham, Chelsea, Manchester City
Bobby Charlton	Manchester United, Preston North End
Ashley Cole	Arsenal, Chelsea, Derby County
Bobby Moore	West Ham, Fulham
Steven Gerrard	Liverpool
David Beckham	Manchester United
Wayne Rooney	Everton, Manchester United, Derby County
Peter Shilton	Leicester City, Stoke City, Nottingham Forest, Southampton, Derby County, Plymouth Argyle, Wimbledon, Bolton Wanderers, Coventry City, West Ham United, Leyton Orient

Caps

· A LITTLE BOOK OF FOOTBALL ·

★ ENGLAND CAPS CHART ★

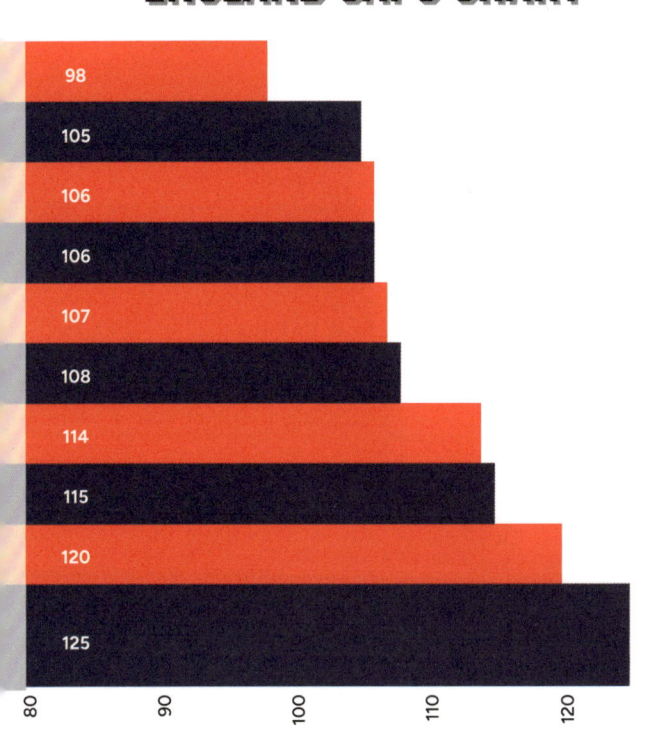

Caps
98
105
106
106
107
108
114
115
120
125

80　90　100　110　120　130

·A LITTLE BOOK OF FOOTBALL·

★ BOBBY MOORE ★

Bobby Moore, West Ham and England's legendary captain, was a talent from a young age with an innate understanding of the physics of the ball. As well as coming through the West Ham youth set-up, Moore played for the Essex youth cricket squad, and had captained and opened the batting for a South against North match alongside nascent fellow England footballer Geoff Hurst in 1956 (who actually went on to make a first-team appearance for Essex in the County Championship in 1962).

In an era where defending tended to be on the robust and assertive side, Moore stood out as an expert in the mechanics of the game, anticipating and disrupting opponents' attacks with precision and finesse.

Take, for example, a little-analysed match on 30 July 1966. It's extra time, the 120th minute. England are clinging on to a one-goal lead, Germany are throwing everyone forward in a desperate pursuit of a goal to bring the score to 3–3 and take the match to penalties.

Moore has the ball, the Wembley crowd are baying for him to take it to the corner flag, put it out of play, anything to use up time and give the Three Lions the victory. Moore, though, kept his head, didn't look to the sidelines, he looked up the pitch, into the German half, where Hurst had acres of clear space. Moore launches the ball forward, half the length of the pitch, virtually to Hurst's feet, Hurst controls it and strides towards the goal …

The only thing wrong with Kenneth Wolstenholme's sublime commentary of that moment is that it doesn't acknowledge the sheer class and composure of Moore's pass. If Moore hadn't found the pass that let Hurst find the net, the arguments about the third goal (see page 41) would still be reverberating around football today. Discount the third goal if you are going to be unsporting; with Moore on the pitch England still won. Moore's foresight made the game safe and the result indisputable.

Moore played for England 108 times over 11 years, a record number of caps at the time, which was only surpassed for an outfield player by David Beckham in 2009, and subsequently Wayne Rooney and Steven Gerrard. (Goalie Peter Shilton had previously taken the record as an overall player.)

Domestically, he led West Ham to the FA Cup in 1963/64, the Charity Shield in 1964/65 and the European Cup

Winners' Cup in 1964/65. Which wasn't a bad warm up for what happened in 1966.

After his 16 years with the Hammers, he moved across London to Fulham before seeing out his playing days with a handful of appearances for various clubs, mostly in the US.

It is also worth noting that while everything about Moore points to him being the kind of clean, upstanding, fair-play kind of a chap that we all aspire to be, he was more than capable of standing his ground if someone tried to take a liberty. He wasn't fast, but he made up for the fact by knowing where he needed to be and, more often than not, getting there before anyone else realised. As Jock Stein, the legendary Scotland manager, said in 1969, "There should be a law against him. He knows what's happening 20 minutes before anyone else."

Moore's contribution to sport and British society as a whole has been recognised repeatedly. He was declared the BBC Sports Personality of the Year in 1966, the first footballer to win the award (it was 24 years before another footballer won the accolade). He was made an OBE in 1967, and in 2002 he not only became an inaugural inductee of the English Football Hall of Fame but was also named on the BBC's list of the 100 Greatest Britons.

• A LITTLE BOOK OF FOOTBALL •

	Appearances	Years active	Clean sheets
Nigel Martyn	23	1992–2002	13
David James	53	1997–2010	21
Paul Robinson	41	2003–2007	24
Chris Woods	43	1985–1993	26
Ray Clemence	61	1972–1983	27
Jordan Pickford	60	2017–present	31
Gordon Banks	73	1963–1972	35
David Seaman	75	1988–2002	40
Joe Hart	75	2008–2017	43
Peter Shilton	125	1970–1990	66

·A LITTLE BOOK OF FOOTBALL·

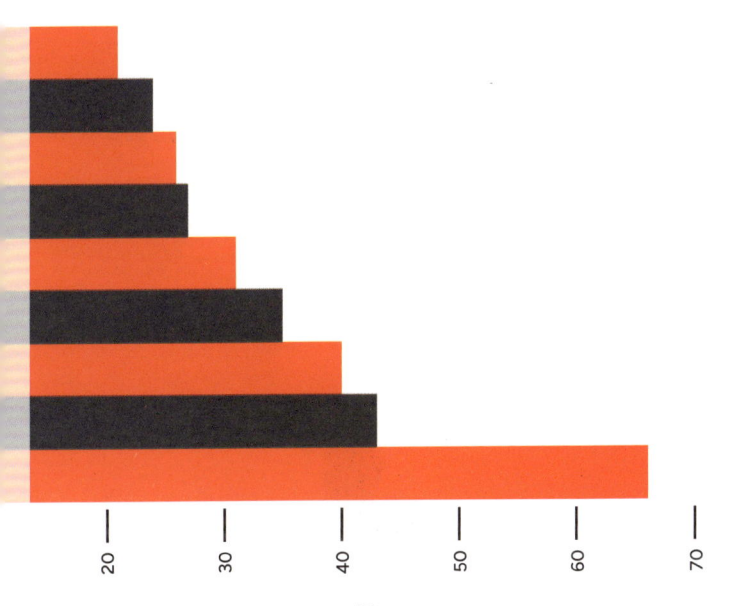

★ ENGLAND CLEAN SHEETS ★

20 30 40 50 60 70

· A LITTLE BOOK OF FOOTBALL ·

★ SIR STANLEY MATTHEWS ★

With some people, often politicians for some reason, society struggles to recognise their knighthoods. Sir Stanley Matthews, known as 'The Wizard of the Dribble', is someone who is automatically given his honorific, no matter what the circumstance. He was the very first European Footballer of the Year, he won the Second Division in both 1932/33 and 1962/63 (let that sink in), he won the Football League War Cup in 1942/43 and the FA Cup in 1952/53. He also won the British Home Championship nine times.

Despite interest from across England after his England Schoolboys debut, Matthews joined Stoke for £1 per week when he reached 15, a wage that rose to £5 per week when he reached 17. By all accounts, he could have signed for any team in the land, but he stuck with Stoke for 15 war-interrupted years, making 259 league appearances, putting the ball in the back of the net 51 times and contributing to many more goals.

While he played throughout World War II in a variety of scratch teams in England and Scotland, the war took Matthews away from his professional career between the ages of 24 and 30. Plenty lost far more, of course, but it's an important period in a player's development and sad to think what the crowds missed.

In total, he played for England 54 times between 1934 and 1957, scoring 11 times. He also played 13 times in the Football League XI and the United Kingdom national football team three times.

He was based near Blackpool during his army days, so when his time at Stoke came to a close shortly after the resumption of professional football, it was natural that he would sign for the Seasiders. He stayed there for 14 years, playing 379 times and contributing 17 goals. He also helped Blackpool win the FA Cup in 1952/53 after a phenomenal final, which came to be known as the 'Matthews final'. With 35 minutes left to play, Bolton were holding a 3–1 lead, but Blackpool turned it round, and by the final whistle the scoreline was 4–3.

He returned to Stoke for the final few years of his playing career, helping them to promotion back to the First Division and winning the Football Writers' Association's Footballer of the Year award for the second time in his career in 1962/63. At 48 years old.

He made his final appearance in the Football League aged 50. While he had an unsatisfying stint in English football management, he enjoyed coaching and spent 25 years bringing football to African children, including in South Africa in defiance of the apartheid regime.

· A LITTLE BOOK OF FOOTBALL ·

> "Scoring is easy.
> You just kick the ball at
> the goal and if God
> and your mother wanted
> you to score that day,
> you will."

Sir Stanley Matthews knew it was all about keeping the right people sweet.

★ THE FIRST FIFA WORLD CUP ★

Towards the end of the 1920s, as football grew into a global phenomenon, the world's football governing body, FIFA, decided to hold a competition in 1930 to decide who was the best team in the world. Football had been a summer Olympic sport since the London games of 1908, but FIFA felt that football was due a spotlight of its own, and the World Cup was born.

Owing to political shenanigans, none of the British teams would participate, and the fact that the endeavour would take players away from their domestic football seasons for three months meant that only four European teams – Belgium, France, Romania and Yugoslavia – could be persuaded to make the trip to Uruguay to compete. Gloriously, all four teams and their entourages travelled together on the same ship which must have been ... interesting. They stopped to pick up Brazil on the way, which was kind.

It is probably fair to say that the competition's teething troubles didn't end with limited European participation. In one match, the ref blew time for the match six minutes early, denying France a clear goal-scoring opportunity. In another, only 2,500 spectators officially turned up (although eyewitnesses suggest the actual number was closer to 300).

Accounts differ about whether there was due to be a play-off to decide third and fourth place. Some say that the match nobody wants to be involved in was not invented until 1934, while others suggest that Yugoslavia were so incensed by the refereeing decisions that they believed cost them their place in the final that they refused to play.

The final was between Argentina and Uruguay, a repeat of the Olympic gold medal match two years previously. The two teams could not agree which ball to use, so ended up playing the first half with the Argentinian choice of ball and the second half with a Uruguayan ball. (Trivia fans might like to know that the two balls in question were the Tiento and the heavier T-Model, respectively.) Argentina won the first half 2–1 but Uruguay recovered with their ball in the second half and went on to win 4–2. They were presented with the first World Cup Trophy by FIFA president Jules Rimet.

The trophy was later named after him, nicked in England in 1966, recovered by a dog, presented to Brazil to celebrate their third World Cup victory in 1970, nicked again – and might be out there, somewhere, still gleaming.

For those who suggest that hooliganism in football has only really existed since the 1970s, it's worth pointing out that after the match in 1930, the Uruguayan embassy in Buenos Aires was pelted with rocks.

It is also worth noting that the next World Cup was held in Europe to try to entice more European teams into being involved. The decision to hold the tournament in Italy, then being ruled by fascist dictator Benito Mussolini, faced criticism because it was felt that football's governing bodies were ignoring significant human rights issues. *'Più le cose cambiano più rimangono le stesse,'** as they say.

> **The first ever World Cup goal, a volley in the 19th minute, was scored by France's Lucien Laurent, playing against Mexico. He saw France lift the 1998 World Cup on home turf aged 91, the only surviving member of that first World Cup team to do so.**

*The more things change, the more they stay the same.

· A LITTLE BOOK OF FOOTBALL ·

"Football is a game you cannot play without making mistakes."

Jurgen Klopp.

·A LITTLE BOOK OF FOOTBALL·

★ GARETH BALE ★

Gareth Bale had a stellar career and is one of the greatest footballing talents to have ever emerged from Wales.

His talent was clear from an early age. At school, his PE teacher implemented a strict one-touch-and-no-left-foot rule so that his classmates would have a chance in games of football against him. Given that 40 of his 53 goals for Tottenham Hotspur came through his left boot, you can see why the rule was necessary.

Bale joined the Southampton youth set-up and spent a season and a bit with them as a professional before moving on to Spurs. He spent six seasons at White Hart Lane, evolving his game to move from a defensive to a midfield position, which enabled him to deliver 22 assists in addition to his 53 goals during his 166 appearances.

He signed for Real Madrid at the start of the 2013/14 season, and was instrumental in helping them win La Liga and the FIFA Club World Cup three times, the UEFA Super Cup twice and the Copa del Rey and the Supercopa de España once each. Oh, and best not forget the Champions League five times. Which is not a bad haul for someone whose career in Spain is perceived as being blighted by injury and missed opportunities.

Between 2006 and 2022, he played for Wales 111 times, finding the net 41 times in the process.

• A LITTLE BOOK OF FOOTBALL •

"I don't go out, so I don't get attention from girls. They're not going to have posters of me on their walls. I just try to get on with my life."

You have to ask if Gareth Bale is actually real.

★ GOAL NETS ★

Sometimes an innovation comes in and we all spend several quiet moments looking at it in awe and wondering why we didn't invent it ourselves. Things that are so helpful, so simple and so obvious that not even football pundits could find a way to argue about them. Case in point: nets in goals.

The FA was formed in 1863 with the aim of standardising the rules of football. The crossbar, initially simply a piece of tape, made its professional debut two years later, in 1885. It was over two decades before someone had the bright idea of putting up a football net — and they weren't mandated until 1891.

So basically, it took more than a quarter of a century of contested goals before someone thought to themselves, how can I:

- ⚽ make it clearer when a goal has been scored

- ⚽ stop managers moaning

- ⚽ stop goalies having to hare off into the park to get the ball back when a goal is scored (it was 15 more years before ballboys were deployed for the task).

The person we have to thank for the invention of the goal net was a civil engineer by the name of John Alexander Brodie, who was also closely involved with the design and building of the Queensway Road Tunnel under the River Mersey, developed the first ring road in the UK, and a string of other projects that have been replicated across the country.

He is said to have been most proud of his contribution to football, though. The story goes that, in 1889, the keen Everton fan was at a match where the Toffees were one down but had a potential equaliser ruled out because the referee couldn't tell if the ball went inside or outside the post. If the goal had been allowed there would have been a completely different complexion on the game. As he stomped off into the night, presumably chuntering darkly about all the injustice that Everton had had to endure down the years — and would continue to do so — he thrust his hands into his pockets. This got him to thinking: if the goal had a pocket that trapped the ball when it went in, there might not ever be any more injustice in football ever again.

It would be nice to say that the goal net Brodie developed has made contentious goal discussions a thing of the past, but the truth of the matter is that even when humanity transcends this meagre physical form and becomes a celestial race of pure thought, it will still find ways to argue about football.

· A LITTLE BOOK OF FOOTBALL ·

"It's end to end stuff, but from side to side."

Trevor Brooking tries to bring the excitement when one team parked the bus.

· A LITTLE BOOK OF FOOTBALL ·

	Appearances	Goals
Vivian Woodwood	23	29
Frank Lampard	106	29
Alan Shearer	63	30
Nat Lofthouse	33	30
Sir Tom Finney	76	30
Michael Owen	89	40
Jimmy Greaves	57	44
Gary Lineker	80	48
Sir Bobby Charlton	106	49
Wayne Rooney	120	53
Harry Kane	89	66

0   10   20

· A LITTLE BOOK OF FOOTBALL ·

★ ENGLAND GOAL SCORERS ★

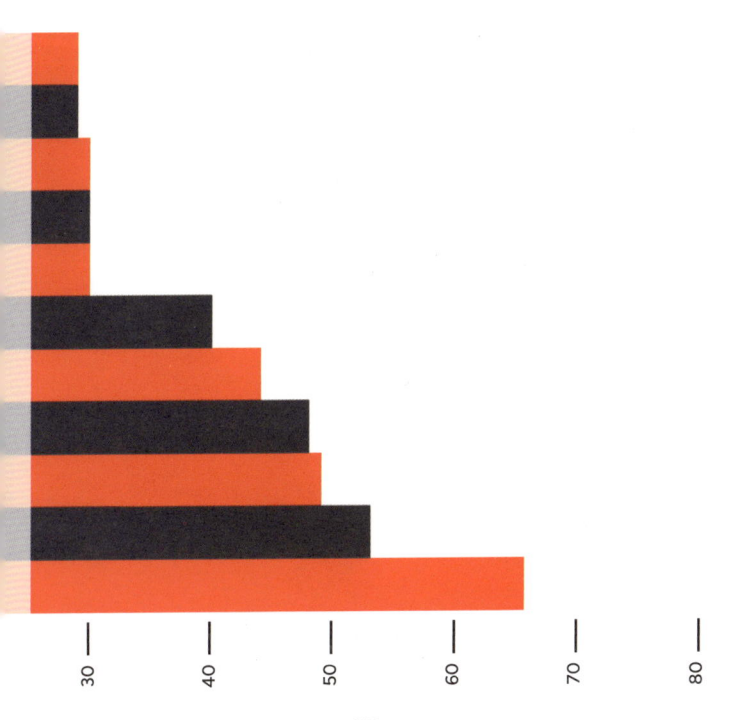

30   40   50   60   70   80

87

·A LITTLE BOOK OF FOOTBALL·

★ DAVID BECKHAM ★

David Beckham probably isn't real. It seems likely that he was created by artificial-intelligence-powered scriptwriting machines to be the perfect icon for English football. Let's look at the facts.

Born in east London, he is said to have come through the Tottenham Academy. Both he and his father were United fans; one of his middle names, Robert, was given to him in honour of Bobby Charlton. So, when United came knocking, the computers generated him a new haircut and he headed north.

Once he got to United, Beckham became part of an unfeasibly talented youth squad that included Nicky Butt, Ryan Giggs, Gary and Phil Neville and Paul Scholes. Together, this plucky band of lads helped take Manchester United to a period of phenomenal success — but it wasn't all plain sailing.

When the 1998 World Cup rolled around, and despite Beckham having a new haircut, the England manager decided against picking him for the first two matches, suggesting that his off-field life was distracting him from his on-field performance. Ultimately, though, the manager bowed to pressure from the press and fans, and our hero was picked for the final group-stage match. Would you believe it, he single-handedly roused the slumbering Three Lions, scored and helped deliver a comfortable victory against Colombia, taking England through to the last 16 by the skin of their teeth.

But then, in the next match against Argentina, he was fouled by Diego Simeone. While lying on the ground, Beckham lashed out at Simeone, who tumbled theatrically to the floor with a chuckle, right in front of the referee. Beckham was given a straight red card. England was incensed. The newspapers were up in arms. How could Beckham have gone from hero to zero so quickly? Michael Owen's phenomenal equalising strike was all but forgotten. Brand Beckham was in serious jeopardy.

Three years and several fresh trims later, Beckham completed his redemption arc as an England player by pretty much single-handedly saving the campaign for qualification for the 2002 World Cup. This included a superb equalising free kick against Greece that got England through. When did the free kick happen? In the last minute. Never mind squeaky-bum time, this was really unlikely-Hollywood-script time.

But it doesn't end there. Back on the domestic scene, there were growing tensions building between Beckham and United's legendary gaffer, Sir Alex Ferguson, who was allegedly sick to the back teeth of the circus that went with having Brand Beckham associated with his team. Ole Gunnar Solskjær's football boot apparently made its way through the Lynx-impregnated air of the Old Trafford changing room at high velocity, propelled by a manager enraged by a perceived lack of effort.

A stitched-up Beckham brushed himself down, got himself a new haircut and headed off to Real Madrid. Many expected him to struggle among Spain's *Galácticos*, but he excelled, making 166 league appearances, scoring 13 times and setting up many more. After that, new haircut, off to America, win the league twice, new haircut, brief sojourn in Paris, win Ligue 1, buy a football club and ride off into the sunset as the credits roll.

The rise, fall, rise, fall and rise again of David Beckham. A global fashion, hairdressing icon and, it should always be remembered, an unreal footballer.

> David Beckham's incredible free kick-taking talent of curling the ball round his opponent's wall is well documented, and even inspired the film *Bend it Like Beckham* in 2023. In total, he scored 65 free kicks for club and country in his career.

· A LITTLE BOOK OF FOOTBALL ·

★ THE BATTLE AT THE BOTTOM ★

There's no doubt, relegation is a brutal way to end the season. Knowing that your team is being consigned to the slightly less glamorous surroundings of the league below can make May a bitter, bitter month. At the same time, though, without relegation there wouldn't be the absolute euphoria of promotion – that moment when your team, your town can look forward to a year playing in the slightly more glamorous surroundings of the league above.

Even as the ecstasy of promotion courses through the town, most teams, most fans, are fairly realistic about their prospects in the coming year. The open-top bus parade down the high street masquerades as a celebration, but everyone lining the streets is looking at the waving, smiling players and quietly trying to work out if they are good enough to play at the level up. Can the club afford anyone better? Is the team good enough to survive or will they just be another one-season wonder?

Delving down into the statistics at the bottom of the table at the end of a season can be a sobering pastime. In the Premier League's three-and-a-bit decades, the average number of points between survival and relegation is three. 39 points is safe, 36 is oblivion. A single game that makes the difference between staying with the glitz and glamour of the top flight, testing your mettle against the very best players in the world, the possibility of European football, and the people around you sighing, shrugging and saying, "Oh well, the Championship's a better league anyway."

Only eight times in 32 years has the gap between safety and relegation been more than three points, so everything's to play for throughout the season. One good day could make the difference.

There may be a scrap for the final relegation place, but it's a different story two places below. At the very foot of the table, the average number of points is a mere 26: 13 points, or nearly five victories, away from the last safe place in the league. Only twice has last place been within a game of safety at the end of the season, and last place has been adrift from safety by more than 15 points more than a third of the time.

Football relegation battles are a truly brutal part of the sport, but at least it means there's something to play for as the season winds down.

· A LITTLE BOOK OF FOOTBALL ·

"I start early and I stay late, day after day, year after year; it took me 17 years and 114 days to become an overnight success."

Lionel Messi, a player who never found hard work too taxing.

⭐ RELEGATED TO HISTORY ⭐

Relegation is horrible, it can be unfair, and it can be massively difficult for a team to pick itself up and get back in the hunt for recovery. But, over the course of the season, it's probably the best way to give everyone, including the teams in the leagues below, an incentive to keep playing to the best of their abilities.

It wasn't always worked out simply on points, though.

Back in the 1890s, before football had really taken off in southern England, there were two main leagues operating across the Midlands and the north. These were specifically the Football Alliance and the FA-backed Football League.

When these two leagues merged in 1892, the teams in the Football League formed the majority of the First Division while the Football Alliance transmuted into the Second Division. There was room to move between the two leagues. So far, so logical.

Where it was different was that while the best teams in the Second Division and worst teams in the First Division could change places, rather than it being decided on the cold, hard logic of points, the teams had to stand for re-election before taking their place in the next season. At the bottom end of the Second Division, non-league clubs could stand for election against any non-league teams that had ambitions.

To make the decision easier, in many of the early seasons there were a series of test matches, which we would probably call play-offs today, between the top two of Second Division and the bottom two of the Second Division. These presumably influenced decisions but weren't always the deciding factor.

Basically, the chairmen (and they were all men, and you know they were all smoking cigars and quaffing only the very finest late-vintage port) of all the football clubs got together, looked at the relegation and promotion places, listened to the pleas of the teams involved, looked at the results of the test matches, quaffed a bit more port and decided who should stay up and who should go down.

The election system was also deployed when the leagues were extended, most infamously in 1919 during an incident that not only soured relations between Tottenham and Arsenal for a century, but also led to the untimely demise of White Hart Lane's resident parrot. Allegedly.

Without getting into the details of the shenanigans between two north London neighbours, the election system carried on for the top two divisions until the 1921/22 season. At this point, everyone realised that there was a far easier way to decide the relegation and promotion places, and that was to look at the relegation and promotion positions at the end of the season. It did, sadly, mean that the chairmen couldn't get together and drink quite as much very fine vintage port, which was sad for them, but that's progress. And they are almost certainly bound to have found other excuses to do so …

The election/re-election system existed at the foot of the Football League until the 1985/86 season, although the chairmen at that level of football presumably had to make do with instant coffee made with powdered milk and possibly a roll-up, rather than port and cigars.

> **Hartlepool United suffered the largest number of re-election campaigns, enduring fourteen tense meetings between 1924 and 1984 – but they were never voted out of the league.**

•A LITTLE BOOK OF FOOTBALL•

★ KENNY DALGLISH ★

• A LITTLE BOOK OF FOOTBALL •

Kenny Dalglish spent the first eight years of his professional career with Celtic, winning four Scottish top-flight titles (awkwardly right at the point where the Scottish Division One became the Premier Division), four Scottish Cups and a Scottish League Cup. From there he followed the well-beaten path between Glasgow and Liverpool, arriving as a direct replacement for Kevin Keegan, who had headed off to Hamburger Sport-Verein to spare Britain more of those wooden Brut-33 adverts. Dalglish helped Liverpool maintain the momentum of their first period of European dominance in the 1970s and 1980s.

And it really was quite a period of dominance. Dalglish helped deliver six English First Division titles, four League Cups, an FA Cup, a Football League Super Cup, a European Super Cup, three Charity Shields and three European Cups. He won three of the First Division titles, two of the FA Cups and two of the FA Charity Shields as Liverpool's player-manager.

He also played 102 times for Scotland, scoring 30 times between 1971 and 1986. He is the most capped Scottish international and is the country's joint highest goal scorer alongside Denis Law.

After moving on from Liverpool (and with his playing days behind him), Dalglish took the reins at Blackburn Rovers, leading them out of the English Second Division into the Premier League at the end of the 1991/92 season and then leading them to the top of the Premier League in 1994/95. He also managed Newcastle United and Celtic (in a caretaker role) before making a brief return as manager of Liverpool.

Dalglish's achievements in football reach far further, but he will always be synonymous with Liverpool. The Centenary Stand at Anfield was renamed as the Sir Kenny Dalglish Stand in his honour in 2017, and he has been inducted into both the English and Scottish Football Halls of Fame.

> King Kenny inspired Alan Bleasdale's 1980s drama *Scully* about a teenage boy dreaming of getting a trial for Liverpool. Dalglish even had a cameo appearance in the dream-like sequences – but the role was originally written for Kevin Keegan, before he left the club.

CORNER FLAGS

In a world of glitter and glamour, it's easy to overlook the humble corner flag. It sits, flapping forlornly in the breeze, overseeing a tiny kingdom, only taking the spotlight on a rare occasion when a goal scorer decides to use it as a prop for a celebration, only commented on when a team decides to use triangular rather than rectangular flags.

Once upon a time, though, the corner flag held the fate of entire games within its grip.

In the early days of football, draws were frowned upon. They were deemed to be an unsatisfying way to end a contest; so, under the rules of some kinds of football, there were goals and there were also things called rouges. Basically, what you had was the goals (with or without a crossbar), but flanking the goals, a few metres on either side, were flags on sticks. If an attacking player took a shot that missed the goal but the ball went out of play on the goal side of these flags, the attacking team would be awarded a rouge. If the match ended in a draw, the number of rouges would be totted up and the win awarded to the team with the most rouges.

It's not a rule that made it into the first edition of the FA's rules in 1863. This is probably a good thing because while it's relatively simple, it's also a lot of faff.

The flags on sticks lived on, though, moving further out of the orbit of the goals, taking up residence at the corners of the pitch where they stand to this day.

Corner flags are usually rectangular but sometimes triangular flags turn up. This isn't just when certain teams are feeling like they want to spice it up a little, there's actually a convention surrounding the FA Cup that says if a team has lifted the trophy they have the right to use triangular flags.

It is said to have grown out of south Wales, where Cardiff reportedly started using triangular flags in 1927 to gently remind their neighbours that they'd lifted the cup. The idea caught on and several teams that have lifted the cup now use triangular flags for FA Cup matches.

It's a convention rather than a rule, though. There's not actually very much in the rule book about corner flags except that they a) have to be there and b) can't be used for advertising. And if you think it's ridiculous to have to stipulate that they can't be used for advertising, then honey, you don't know the Premier League.

· A LITTLE BOOK OF FOOTBALL ·

★ VALUE AT RISK: ★
FOOTBALL AND THE VAR DEBATE

One of the key reasons that football has swept across all the corners of the globe is that it has a core principle: the game is basically the same, whether it's being played in a shabby urban park in front of one man and his dog or on the expertly manicured turf of one of the world's great stadiums in front of an audience of millions.

At any level beyond a kick-about with your mates, the referee stands at the centre of it all, making split-second decisions. Was that offside? Did the ball cross the line? How many feet were involved in that tackle? Was there intent? Was that dissent? Have a word, produce the yellow or brandish the red? There's a lot of pressure resting on those black-clad shoulders ...

And sometimes they get it wrong.

Now, it's annoying when a ref gets it wrong in a Sunday league match, but it can be devastating when a mistake is made at the top level – a single bad decision can break a season, cost millions of pounds and change the fate of entire communities.

So, for the 2019/20 season of the English Premier League it was decided to bring in the Video Assistant Referee (VAR) system. It took the game away from the principle of simplicity, but it was thought to be worth it if it helped referees and cut down some of the infinite moaning on *Match of the Day* …

… which it has not.

Half of infinity is still infinity

Part of the joy of any sport is that it gives people something to moan about; like it or not, moaning is a key part of the human condition. Moan about it all you like, it's still true.

VAR has undoubtably suffered teething troubles. Hopefully, these will be ironed out, but even in the unlikely event that it becomes perfect, it still creates a bigger problem: time.

Stadiums are filled – week in, week out – by people who want to come together and enjoy the bedlam on the terraces that follows the ball being walloped into the back of the net. The striker wheels around, their team mobs them and there's pandemonium in the stands. That release of endorphins is what people come for.

The problem at the moment is that a lot of goals are checked by VAR, creating a pause before the celebration. It's a pause that takes away the glorious moment of catharsis. It's the right thing to do, but it sucks out the emotion.

We'd better head off

There's also an issue for the travelling fans. As football has gradually moved away from the 3:00 pm Saturday slot, matches now take place late on Sunday afternoons and on weeknights. As things stand, games in the Premier League are having around six minutes of time added on at the end of each half, which translates to an extra 15 minutes per match. This doesn't make much difference for fans watching at home or down the local, but if you've made the effort to get to the stadium to watch the match, soak up the atmosphere and join in the singing, that 15 minutes can be a problem.

Fans have to get home for work the next day, so they need to get to their trains. Basically, we are getting to the point where it's 3–3 in the 92nd minute, your team has an attack and you've got to head for the exit. You can hear the crowd cheer as you walk off into the night and check your phone to find out if there was a goal, but you still missed it. It might have been better to have saved your money and watched it at home.

In principle, VAR might be a good thing; in practice, it's holding up the game, diluting the celebrations and could be making people think twice about going to a match. That might not be great for football in the long term.

> In the 2023/24 Premier League season, VAR caused a total of 110 referee decisions to be overturned, versus only 2 rejected overturns. This led to 33 goals being allowed and 50 disallowed; 28 penalties being awarded and 12 penalties being overturned; and 32 goals ruled out for offside and 7 goals awarded after incorrect offside. It also led to 13 red cards and 1 overturned red card.

· A LITTLE BOOK OF FOOTBALL ·

"Look, I'm a coach, I'm not Harry Potter. He is magical, but in reality there is no magic. Magic is fiction and football is real."

José Mourinho speaking during his mundane spell as manager of Real Madrid.

·A LITTLE BOOK OF FOOTBALL·

★ ALAN SHEARER ★

Always a threat, always smiling when he found the goal, Alan Shearer's also an unusual example of a player who rose to footballing prominence in the modern game despite never playing for one of the major clubs of the era, either in England or abroad.

There are a lot of elements to his professional footballing career. He was tough, clearly hard working, an exceptional leader for club and country, and had the intelligence to evolve the way he played football as he got older.

He spent the first four years of his professional career at Southampton before joining Blackburn Rovers, where he scored 16 times in his first 21 games, including two on debut. His goals helped Blackburn come fourth in their first season after promotion and second the year after that — before they took the Premier League title in 1994/95.

Maintaining a team that can challenge at the top level is an expensive business, though, and while Real Madrid expressed an interest and Manchester United had a formal bid for the striker rejected at the start of July 1996 (with Blackburn insisting that the striker was not for sale), three weeks later, he was away to his boyhood club — Newcastle United — for a hefty fee.

He stayed with Newcastle for the rest of his playing career, making 303 league appearances for the Magpies over 10 years. In total, he made 441 appearances in the Premier League, delivering 260 goals, and 64 assists. He also won the Premier League Golden Boot for three consecutive years.

He scored in his full England debut against France, going on to deliver 30 goals across 63 appearances for the Three Lions. He wore the captain's armband 34 times.

But the main thing that you get from watching Shearer in his prime is how much fun he seemed to be having. He had an infectious grin that brought enjoyment to the terraces (although he appears to have wound up the likes of Roy Keane on occasion).

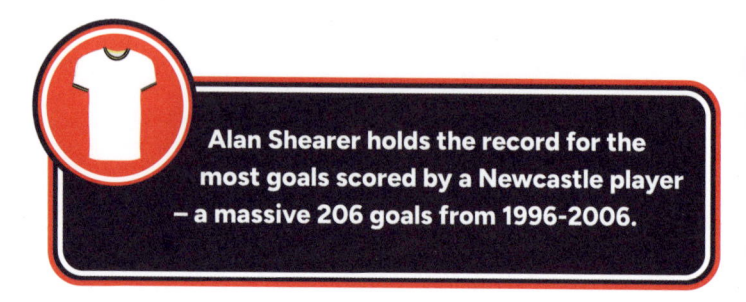

> Alan Shearer holds the record for the most goals scored by a Newcastle player – a massive 206 goals from 1996-2006.

★ DUGOUTS ★

Football is an ever-changing beast, with new ideas, formations and training techniques falling into and out of fashion almost as quickly as the flared jeans and kipper ties so beloved by footballers in the 1970s. These days, at the top levels at least, managers and their staff oversee their teams from well-appointed technical areas, resplendent with leatherette seats that probably have a massage function if you can find the right button.

These technical areas are still sometimes called dugouts, and there's a simple reason for this: back in the 1930s, there was a fashion for lowering the seating level so that managers could watch their players' footwork throughout the game.

Baseball takes a similar approach, but football dugouts came into the game not from looking west to America but from looking north-east to Norway.

A fellow by the name of David Coleman, who spent his playing days at Motherwell, Aberdeen, Dumbarton and for Scotland, wanted to develop the game. As he started to move into management, he looked for inspiration from other countries' training techniques and set-ups. This led him to spend a few summers working with SK Brann in Bergen, Norway, where the managers positioned themselves in open-fronted huts that let them communicate with their players but also shelter from the elements. Norway's weather, it should be noted, is very pleasant in the summer, but there are another nine months in the year.

Coleman wanted his players to adopt an open, possession-based style of play, and when he was appointed as coach to Aberdeen, he created a covered, sunken area by the touchline where he could watch his players' footwork at eye level without being too exposed to the elements. Aberdeen's weather, it should be noted, is very pleasant in the summer, but there are another eleven-and-a-half months in the year.

This was in 1934; a few years later, Everton came to visit Pittodrie Park, thought the idea was a good one and took it south, where it spread widely.

The technical area was clearly delineated in an update to FIFA's rules in 1993, at around the same time as technical teams and managers' coats had begun to grow too large to be confined by the traditional dugout. Dugouts fell out of fashion, but the word lives on, at least in article headlines, where it's just that little bit snappier than 'technical area'.

Football is a game that brings joy, and nowhere is that joy clearer than in the moments after someone scores. Peter Crouch's robot celebration probably gets it about right: it's funny, self-effacing and relatively short. Lionel Messi, Christiano Ronaldo, Kylian Mbappé and Emile Heskey all have iconic celebrations that everyone recognises and show up all the time on social media. Having a team launch into an intricate piece of choreography to celebrate a goal is generally a bit annoying: if you've got time to work on a dance move, perhaps you should look at how many better ways you could spend your time. So, it's no surprise that various football associations around the world have rules in place about time wasting and generally going over the line into the realm of pillock.

It's a fine line though. If the rules are too rigid and prescriptive, some bright spark will find a loophole and drive a coach and horses through it. Potentially literally, given half a chance. It's also virtually impossible to create rules that will account for the sheer stupidity of some players when it comes to celebrating. A recent match in Italy saw a player sent off for celebrating after they scored and then ran over to the dugout, headbutted the side and shattered the plexiglass. Now you might suggest that the ref was a bit mean sending the player off, but really, someone's got to clear that up, and someone else has to pay for it.

· A LITTLE BOOK OF FOOTBALL ·

★ A BRIEF HISTORY OF BALLS ★

And so we roll around, as we inevitably would, to the sphere at the centre of it all, the second syllable in the word itself, the one item that the game can never do without: the ball.

There are many games played around the world that can claim to be an ancestor of what we call football today: games played with rubber balls, games played with cured animal bladders, games played with human skulls. The ball that we use today, though, is most directly descended from a cow, pig or sheep's inflated bladder. At some point, in the nebulously titled medieval times, it started to gain a leather covering to increase its longevity and make headers marginally less unpleasant.

Vulcanised rubber came along in the 1850s, usurping the bladder as the central part of the sphere. Rubber had several benefits, namely:

- ⚽ it bounced better than an animal's bladder
- ⚽ it held its shape better than an animal's bladder
- ⚽ it was considerably less grim than an animal's bladder.

Live long and bounce

Vulcanised rubber arrived on the scene just as the FA was starting to standardise the rules of football across Britain and it enabled the ball to be standardised into pretty much the size and weight that we know today. Interestingly, the football's first set of rules did not specify the size of the ball, but the 1872 revision stated that a football should be 68–70 cm and 410–450 grams (obviously back in the day it was some inches and a few stone). This is still the specification for an adult size 5 ball.

That was where it was at for the next 70 years, with a few minor tweaks. This wasn't because the balls didn't have problems. On wet days (unusual in Britain, but it never hurts to take them into account), the leather of the ball would get gradually heavier as the game progressed – and there are also plenty of stories about people being left battered and bloody from connecting with the classic ball's prominent stitching.

Release the pressure

Things were made a little better with the addition of a layer of cloth between the rubber and leather sections of the ball in the 1940s. Smaller valves meant that the stitching on the outside could be retired, and waterproof synthetic coverings and inner stitching made the ball more consistent and performance started to be less influenced by the weather. Even so, it was still a heavy brown object that was almost as capable of damage as a sliding defender with mal intent.

When television started to emerge in the 1950s, a further problem started to become apparent: brown balls don't show up against muddy fields on black and white tellies. Both orange and white balls started creeping in, most famously, around these parts at least, for the 1966 World Cup, where their bright colour made it abundantly clear that that third goal in the Final very clearly bounced over the line.

The Telstar goes orbital

Give a child a crayon and ask them to draw a car, and you'll end up with a box on a couple of circles. Ask them to draw a house, and they will proudly give you a box with a triangle on top. Ask them to draw a football, and they will produce a mathematical miracle, a perfect sphere comprising 12 black pentagonal and 20 white hexagonal panels.

An icon of football, the Adidas Telstar was introduced for the 1970 World Cup and has since become the Platonic ideal of what a football should look like. Better balls have been created since, but there has never been such a quantum leap in consistency and durability.

Named after a similarly shaped communications satellite that ushered in the age of instant communications when it was launched in 1962, the Telstar's alternating colours made it easier for players, fans in the stands and all the people back home to see how the ball was moving across the pitch. It is said that only 20 Telstars were used during the 1970 World Cup, but 600,000 replicas were subsequently sold worldwide.

Jabulani and vuvuzela

Since the all-conquering Telstar, the technology that goes into footballs has continued to leap forward, although the enhancements have tended to be less outwardly dramatic. Advances in manufacturing processes mean that balls tend to have fewer than the Telstar's 32 panels, which make the ball soft, strong and able to be kicked a very long way.

That said, it's worth quickly mentioning the 2010 World Cup ball – the Jabulani – which reduced the number of panels to eight – in theory making it lighter, faster and more predictable. In reality, it weaved through the air dramatically and, as a result, was deeply unpopular. Its only fan was Diego Forlán, who got hold of the ball early and spent three months practising with it before the tournament so he could understand its dynamics. He was named the tournament's best player as a result.

The 2010 World Cup also suffered from the massed chorus of vuvuzela, two-foot-long horns that produce a droning noise that local fans inexplicably mistook for good fun. It's hard to tell whether the Jabulani, the vuvuzela or Frank Lampard's disallowed goal was the least popular thing about the tournament.

Balls of the future

Modern balls are lighter, which is hoped will go some way to reducing some of the long-term damage that players are said to have suffered in the past as a result of repeatedly heading a cold, wet lump of rubber and leather.

These days, balls are being constructed out of synthetic leather that is designed at a molecular level, ensuring that energy is passed consistently from the player's foot to the ball whenever the two come into contact.

It's tempting to suggest that with balls being constructed under a microscope, there will never be another period of dramatic innovation, that the future of football development will simply be a steady, flat road of gradual improvements ... Football fans for the last century and a half probably thought the same just before the next bright spark made something phenomenal happen. The emoji for football will always be a Telstar, though.

• A LITTLE BOOK OF FOOTBALL •

"We must have had 99 per cent of the game. It was the other 3 per cent that cost us the match."

Ruud Gullit: Master tactician, sub-average mathematician.

HOME NATIONS FOOTBALL

England/Wales

England and Wales have been married for nearly 800 years. There have been ups and downs within that time, but they basically rub along well together so long as each stay in their lane and keeps the stereotyping to a minimum. Basically, most of the time there's no particular needle when the pair face off for an international game of football.

The other reason is the difference in population size. Some superlative footballers have come out of Wales, but depth of squad has sometimes been a challenge in comparison with England and the statistics tend to reflect this.

Ripping off the sticking plaster, England have won around two thirds of the 104 matches that the two teams have played, with Wales winning a little over 10% of the time. Draws represent the balance, with nil-nils kept at a relatively rare 6%.

The gap between the two teams has got wider over the last few years: the last time that Wales beat England was in 1984.

England/Scotland

The British Isles are steeped in history; some of it good, some of it bad, much of it between England and Scotland. That history has often seeped onto the football pitch, adding an extra spice to any of the 116 occasions the two teams have met so far.

The rights and wrongs of history need not concern us in a light-hearted book about football, so let's just stick to the data and avoid pages and pages of he beheaded/she beheaded.

So here are the footballing facts: England and Scotland have faced each other 116 times to date, with England claiming the glory a little over 40% of the time and Scotland doing the jig around 35% of the time. It's usually a high-scoring fixture, with an average of more than 3.25 goals per match and a nearly 25% chance of five or more goals. On the other side of that, only 3% of games deliver a 0-0 draw (and even then, there's usually plenty to talk about on the way home).

One of those 0-0 draws was the very first official international football match, which was held between the two teams in November 1872 at the West of Scotland Cricket Ground in Glasgow. From such small acorns did the mighty World Cup grow.

Scotland/Wales

Britian is a relatively small island and usually when countries are confined to relatively small spaces, there tends to be tension, but geography and history have conspired to mean there is very little beef between Scotland and Wales. When they do get together it's fairly businesslike and tends to involve less eye rolling in the direction of their joint neighbour to the south/east than their joint neighbour to the south/east would like to think.

The two teams have faced each other 105 times to date, with Scotland taking the honours around 60% of the time and Wales around 20% of the time. They tend to be relatively high scoring affairs, with more than five goals finding the back of the net more than a quarter of the time, and only 5% of the matches deflating to a nil-nil, presumably because an international is always an occasion and people play up most of the time.

Interestingly, Scotland have only won once in the six times that the two teams have met since 1997, although they've not faced each other for more than a decade.

REPUBLIC OF IRELAND

The Republic of Ireland is also part of the British Isles with a rich footballing history of its own, although the beautiful game also has to compete with Rugby Union, Gaelic Football and Hurling for both fans and competitors. Population-wise, the country is slightly larger than Scotland and around twice that of Wales but only around 10% of England. The country has delivered several world class players down the years though, including Roy Keane, Robbie Keane, John O'Shea and Denis Irwin.

Politics has limited the number of times that England and Ireland have faced each other on the football field, with the two teams drawing more than half of the time they meet, England winning just over a third of the time and Ireland coming out on top just over 10% of the time. Honours are fairly even with Scotland, but it turns out that Wales are the team Ireland suffer under the most, losing over 40% of the time, drawing around a quarter of the time and winning just under a third of the time.

It's interesting to note that Manchester had a large Irish population at the time that football was developing as a game, which is part of the reason why there is still a strong affinity between Manchester United and Ireland.

· A LITTLE BOOK OF FOOTBALL ·

Year	Winner(s)
1930	Guillermo Stábile (Argentina)
1934	Oldřich Nejedlý (Czechoslovakia)
1938	Leônidas (Brazil)
1950	Ademir (Brazil)
1954	Sándor Kocsis (Hungary)
1958	Just Fontaine (France)
1962	Flórián Albert (Hungary), Garrincha (Brazil), Valentin Ivanov (Soviet Union), Dražan Jerković (Yugoslavia), Leonel Sánchez (Chile), Vavá (Brazil)
1966	Eusébio (Portugal)
1970	Gerd Müller (Germany)
1974	Grzegorz Lato (Poland)
1978	Mario Kempes (Argentina)
1982	Paolo Rossi (Italy)
1986	Gary Lineker (England)
1990	Salvator Schillachi (Italy)
1994	Oleg Salenko (Russia), Hristo Stoichkov (Bulgaria)
1998	Davor Šuker (Croatia)
2002	Ronaldo (Brazil)
2006	Miroslav Klose (Germany)
2010	Diego Forlan (Uruguay), Thomas Müller (Germany), Wesley Sneijder (Netherlands), David Villa (Spain)
2014	James Rodríguez (Colombia)
2018	Harry Kane (England)
2022	Kylian Mbappé (France)

· A LITTLE BOOK OF FOOTBALL ·

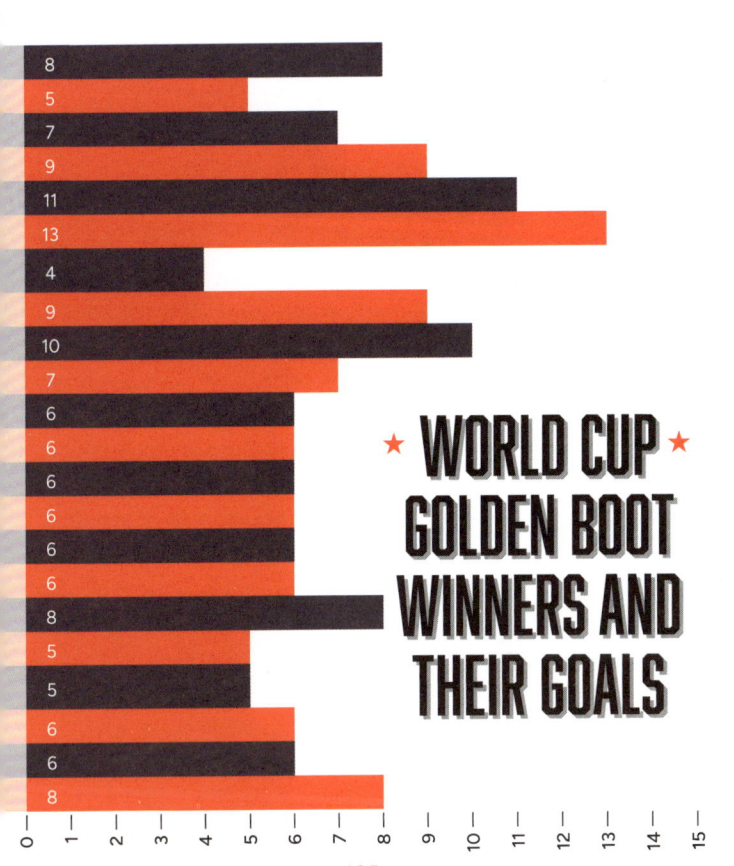

★ WORLD CUP ★ GOLDEN BOOT WINNERS AND THEIR GOALS

• A LITTLE BOOK OF FOOTBALL •

★ THE RECORD-BREAKING ★ 2006/07 SEASON

When you are a fan of a team outside of the big six, you live in hope, but kind of know what to expect. The excitement of a shiny new season; the potential that the new striker will adjust quickly to life in the Premier League; basking in August's full glory, the T-shirts and squinting against the sun ... which quickly fades into an early, grinding winter. The strikers moaning on social media about their difficulty adapting to the culture. A single point from a 0–0 draw is something to celebrate. A quick look at the table isn't quick because it involves a lot of scrolling down.

The 2006/07 season delivered two record-breaking matches involving four teams that are all too familiar with the dotted line at the bottom of the Premier League table.

The first came when Reading ventured down the M3 to Portsmouth. The hosts went up after six minutes and doubled their lead in the 37th minute, but Reading found the net at the psychologically important moment at the end of the first half and then pulled themselves level three minutes into the second.

Pompey then went ahead again, and then, in a breathtaking 20 minutes of football, Reading missed a penalty, Pompey scored a fourth and then a fifth, Reading scored a third, suffered an own goal, before Portsmouth scored a penalty and rounded out the afternoon with an own goal.

The match ended 7–4, and 11 goals remains the highest number scored in a Premier League match. The heartbreaking thing for Reading fans is that they were relegated at the end of the season on goal difference. It might not have worked out anyway, but if they hadn't shipped those extra three goals, they might have avoided the drop.

Meanwhile, in mid-December, Blackburn Rovers' Roque Santa Cruz and Wigan Athletic's Marcus Bent delivered hat-tricks when Wigan beat Blackburn in a 5–3 stunner. This is the only time in Premier League history that both sides in a match have scored a hat-trick.

One other fact that jumps out about the 2006/07 season: the biggest home win was a scintillating 8–1 match between Middlesborough and Manchester City. It was played at the Riverside and City didn't win, which just goes to show how the world has turned.

★ FLOODLIGHTS ★

It's hard to imagine a football world without floodlights, because without floodlights, there'd be no Monday night football, no Champions League football, no Wednesday, Thursday or Friday night football. You could have matches kicking off between about 9:00 am and 3:00 pm, but only at the weekends if you wanted to attract many fans through the turnstiles.

Floodlights started to be introduced into football in 1878, first lighting up the dank Yorkshire evenings at Sheffield United's Bramall Lane, and followed soon after by Blackburn and Darwen. It was exciting to be able to hold matches in the evening, but without a national electricity grid, the lights required batteries and dynamos to work, which had the tendency of making them unreliable.

Nobody had really worked out how to keep the lights in place. According to one report of a Nottingham Forest match played under floodlights in 1889, the high winds meant that the floodlights were being blown around and the neighbouring fields were getting better illumination than the match.

The other challenge, of course, is that at the end of the 19th century the brightest light bulb is estimated to have produced around 50,000 lumens, was around the size of a domestic oven and probably cost a similar amount; these days, you can pick up a head torch for £20 that kicks out around the same level of light. Presumably, the modern bulbs don't get as warm, though, so it's not all progress on a cold winter's night.

Unfortunately, football's governing bodies, mainly comprising football club chairmen, were not really in favour of floodlights. They wanted to keep football's focus on Saturday at 3:00 pm, reasoning that it would enable teams to maximise gate receipts which, in turn and by happy coincidence, would enable chairmen to maximise profit, which, naturally, would always be reinvested in the club.

The only recorded exception to this rule happened just after World War I, when the Dick, Kerr Ladies team wanted to play a charity match in support of former servicemen at Deepdale, the home of Preston North End, in December 1920. It was decided to make it an evening match, and the organisers managed to blag two anti-aircraft searchlights and the appropriate generators to light the game. The ball was painted white so that it stood out under the floodlights.

It didn't catch on, though, and it wasn't until the 1930s that they started to be discussed again. Legendary Arsenal manager and football innovator Herbert Chapman, inspired by a fact-finding mission to Europe where floodlights were commonly used, had them installed at Highbury. It was still another two decades before playing under artificial light was officially sanctioned.

Historians have recently discovered that Caledonian, one of the clubs that transmogrified into Inverness Caledonian Thistle in the 1990s, was one of the first teams to have floodlights in the Highlands of Scotland in the 1930s (who knew they had electricity back then?) Fascinatingly, these floodlights only lasted a few matches because they were repurposed to become part of the hunt for the Loch Ness Monster. It might sound silly, but a reward of £20,000 had been offered for Nessie's capture, which was probably a touch more than the prize money being offered by the Highland Football League at the time.

"When I score, I don't celebrate because it's my job. When a postman delivers letters, does he celebrate?"

Mario Balotelli, a player who at no point had a special T-shirt printed out with the message 'Why always me?' to show in the event of scoring a goal.

· A LITTLE BOOK OF FOOTBALL ·

★ THIERRY HENRY ★

Thierry Henry's career got underway at Arsène Wenger's Monaco, where he played out on the left wing and helped bring a Ligue 1 title to the microstate on the French Riviera. After five years, he moved on to Juventus, but found the defensive mindset of the Italian game stifling, so when the chance came to rejoin Wenger at Arsenal, he pretty much jumped on the first flight to London.

There were plenty who suggested Wenger had spent a lot of money on an obscure player who had hardly lit up Serie A and who would struggle to show his silky skills and finesse in the English game. It's fair to say that Henry proved the doubters wrong, moving in from the wing and becoming one of the most devastating strikers that the Premier League has ever witnessed. Over 258 appearances, he scored 175 goals and made 74 assists, won the Premier League Golden Boot for four seasons and was Player of the Season twice. He also won the title, the FA Cup and the Community shield twice each and was the lynchpin of Arsenal's invincible season.

He spent eight seasons with Arsenal during his first stint there, heading off to Barcelona in 2007 and the New York Red Bulls three years later. He rounded out his playing days with a four-match coda back at Arsenal in 2012.

He enjoyed a similarly storied career with the French national team, winning the World Cup in 1998 and the European Championship in 2000. In total he made 123 appearances for his country, scoring 51 times.

Henry brought creativity and talent to the football pitch, showing what was possible and making the game more beautiful in the process. Before him, English football tended to be a battle of knights with broad swords, slugging it out with heavy blows until one side overpowered the other. Henry had an assassin's eye and a fencer's finesse, creating peril from all over the pitch. You never knew where his attacks would come from, and the game became better as a result.

· A LITTLE BOOK OF FOOTBALL ·

"When he ran past you, it was like trying to chase after someone on a motorbike."

Liverpool's Jamie Carragher reflects on trying to catch Arsenal's Thierry Henry when he hit his stride.

• A LITTLE BOOK OF FOOTBALL •

"Football is the most important of the less important things in the world."

Carlo Ancelotti enjoys football more than going to the supermarket or eating toast.

THREE POINTS FOR A WIN

There are a lot of things in life that took a long time to be introduced but seem utterly obvious when you think about them. Three points for a win is right up there. The thing is, though, three points for a win didn't become part of the game in England until 1981, and even then, it wasn't until the 1994 World Cup in the US that three points was adopted on the world stage.

The person we have to thank for championing the three-point system that we take for granted today is none other than Fulham player and director, Coventry City manager and director, *Match of the Day* anchor and lyricist of the 1971 Arsenal song 'Good old Arsenal', Jimmy Hill.

In the original rules of the game, teams were awarded two points for a win, one for a draw and the other thing for a loss. In Hill's analysis, this tended to encourage teams to play for a draw because, well, there's only a point in it. The problem was that no one really wants to give up their Saturday afternoon if the odds of a strategic 0–0 are high, and by the late 1970s, crowds at football were starting to dry up.

Hill led a working party of football club chairmen who decided that the simplest way to get teams to go for it was to change the stakes. Make it better to pull out all the stops and go for a win than park the bus and be satisfied with a draw.

This is football, so the world is awash with statistics and analysis about whether there have been more or fewer draws in the years since the three-point system was put into effect. Without going too deep into the weeds, it seems likely the impact may not have been all that significant. Potentially banning back passes has been as important in speeding the game up.

It's true about the Arsenal song, by the way. No one's quite sure why, though.

A LITTLE BOOK OF FOOTBALL

★ THE MOST NOTORIOUS DRAW ... ★

It's a fair-sized irony that Jimmy Hill is also responsible for one of the most notorious draws in the history of English football. At the business end of the 1976/77 season, Bristol City, Coventry City and Sunderland were locked in the unusual position of scrapping it out in the final match of the season to avoid relegation.

All three teams were level on points, but Coventry's goal difference put them in the most precarious position. They were playing Bristol at home while Sunderland were away at Everton.

Kick-off approached and everyone associated with the three clubs presumably had butterflies in their stomachs ... This was extra squeaky-bum time.

Hill, then operating as Coventry's managing director, is said to have contrived to have the Coventry match delayed by 10 minutes, apparently claiming crowd congestion. "Chinny reckon," as the kids in the playground said at the time. This seemingly innocuous move meant that Coventry and Bristol would know the result of the Sunderland match by the end of their own contest and could finesse their strategies accordingly.

The match eventually got underway and Coventry strode to a 2–0 lead, but by the 80th minute, Bristol had pegged them back and the match was finely balanced at 2–2. Bristol, though, were by all accounts in the ascendancy and looked most likely to bag themselves a third goal to ensure their safety. As the game ended at Everton, Sunderland had shipped two goals without reply: the Black Cats faced the drop unless Coventry conceded.

At which point, allegedly, Hill raced from the directors' suite to the commentary box and had them announce over the public address system that Sunderland had lost to Everton (there were no live updates on mobile phones back in the day). Hearing this, the players on the pitch realised that a draw was good enough for both teams, that if either of them pushed for a goal they could get hit on the break. The contest, you will be astonished to hear, fizzled out.

According to reports, fans at the stadium were treated to a 10-minute masterclass in passing between defenders. Each back pass (legal back then) was cheered loudly. Bristol players were berated by fans on both sides if they were foolish enough to try to make their way into Coventry's half with the ball. At full time, 2–2 meant Bristol and Coventry survived. The Black Cats were cast out.

Hill's role in the day's shenanigans was commented on in the papers the next day and the sport's highest authorities were so incensed that he was given a formal reprimand. It was written down on a piece of paper they were so cross. Which he presumably accepted with a philosophical shrug as his team stayed up in the top flight.

Hill is widely respected across England for his contributions to football, but he had to tread carefully in certain parts of the north-east until he passed away in 2015 at the ripe old age of 87.

> **As chairman of the Professional Footballers' Association, Hill successfully campaigned for the abolition of the players' maximum wage. As the 60s started to hit their rhythm, money started to flow into football but players were getting precious little of it, with a maximum weekly wage being only £20 per week. Johnny Haynes, one of Hill's Fulham teammates, became the game's first £100-a-week player as a result.**

·A LITTLE BOOK OF FOOTBALL·

★ HARRY KANE ★

Harry Kane has gone through his first season with Bayern Munich without lifting a trophy. This is unfortunate because one of his primary reasons for leaving Tottenham Hotspur at the start of the 2023/24 season was the fact that this generation's most prolific English goal scorer has never lifted significant silverware for club or country. What makes it doubly unfortunate is that the 2023/24 season was the first in 12 where the Bavarian side didn't win the Bundesliga.

Irrespective, there is no doubt that Kane is a superb talent. As a youngster, he spent a year with the Arsenal academy but was released, and subsequently had trials with Tottenham and Watford before being invited to join the Spurs setup, where he impressed by working hard on his fitness and tactical nous.

He signed fully with Spurs at 16 and spent the next couple of years working his way through the ranks and going out on loan to hone his skills. He made his first Premier League start at the back end of the 2013/14 season, scoring in three consecutive matches before announcing his arrival as a fully fledged football player with 21 goals in 34 appearances and a Professional Footballers' Association Young Player of the Year award for 2014/15.

In total, he spent 14 years with Tottenham, making 317 appearances and scoring 213 goals, but while he had a clutch of Premier League Golden Boots and Player of the Year awards, genuine silverware eluded him. After a couple of unsettled, but still prolific, seasons, he moved to Germany.

He has also become captain of an England team that is genuinely felt to be in contention for international tournaments. After nearly 60 years of hurt for the men's game, the ultimate prize would be to win an international competition and go from being a Tottenham to an England legend.

> **A little-known fact is that Harry Kane is a huge NFL fan - he even named his dog after his favourite player, Tom Brady.**
>
> "He reminded me of me," Kane has said. "Brady believed in himself so much - and he kept just working and working, almost obsessively, in order to get better." Kane has also said he would love to become an NFL player once he's retired from proper football.

· A LITTLE BOOK OF FOOTBALL ·

"The game of football is like a canvas, and it's up to the players to paint the most beautiful picture."

Diego Maradona often painted …

Wait for it …

Wait for it …

… with his hands!

• A LITTLE BOOK OF FOOTBALL •

"Success is not just about winning trophies, it's about making a positive impact on the world."

Didier Drogba.

★ SHIRT NUMBERS ★

Shirt numbers are another one of those things that you look at and say, "Well, duh. Why wouldn't you?" – but they weren't actually required in football until the end of the 1930s, around 60 years after the game started to coalesce into its current form. This means that they've been used in football for less than a century.

To be fair, 100 years is a fairly large number, but it's still relatively recent in the big scheme of things.

It is widely claimed, mostly by Arsenal supporters, that it was Arsenal's legendary manager and all-round innovation machine Herbert Chapman who championed the use of shirt numbers, and that Arsenal were the first team to wear shirt numbers in the top flight of English football at the start of the 1928/29 season. The reality is that Chelsea also turned out in numbered shirts on the same day when they played Swansea Town – the only difference being that Chelsea didn't put a number on their goalie (and Chelsea weren't technically in the top flight of English football at the time).

Away from the squabbles and posturing of north and west London football teams, the historical record (such as it is when a monarch isn't involved) suggests that shirt numbers were first used in sports in Australia during a game of rugby union as far back as 1897. The word on the street is that Queensland were hosting New Zealand and shirts were numbered so that the referee, who only knew the local lads, could identify who was doing what. Rugby can be an unnecessarily complicated sport, but there's sometimes some logic behind it all.

Back in the more rational world of football, shirt numbers were initially confined to 1–11 with goalies generally (but not exclusively) taking the number 1 shirt, and the numbers gradually getting higher as you moved up the pitch.

The formal introduction of substitutes into the English game in 1958 changed the simplicity of the 1–11 numbering system, and squads gradually inflated over the next few decades. The mandatory use of 1–11 wasn't actually dropped until 1993, when squad numbers that last for the season were formally adopted.

Argentina went though a phase of numbering the national squad alphabetically in the 1970s and early 1980s, with several outfield players, including Spur's legend Osvaldo 'Ossie' Ardiles, playing in the number 1 shirt during internationals. When fellow Spurs legend Edgar Davids became player-manager of Barnet for the 2013/14 season, he gave himself the number 1 shirt. He said it was in the hope of starting a trend, but six months later he was looking for fresh opportunities elsewhere – and 10 years on, even the good folk of Barnet have probably forgotten that particular piece of trivia ...

> **Players have often used shirt numbers for eccentric reasons. Ronaldo wore number 99 for AC Milan because his teammate Filippo Inzaghi already wore Ronaldo's favoured number 9. Nicklas Bendtner, who played for Arsenal and Sunderland, wore the number 52 as the digits added up to his favourite number. Bruno Guimaraes, the Newcastle Utd midfielder, wears his father's old taxi dispatch number – 39. And Bixente Lizarazu, the French international, chose 69 to match his weight (69kg), height (169cm) and birth year (1969).**

•A LITTLE BOOK OF FOOTBALL•

★ WHY THE GAME IS ★ ALWAYS EVOLVING

Some of football's detractors claim that it has become one of the world's pre-eminent sports simply because it achieved some sort of popular critical mass, but there's probably a bit more to it than that.

Football has also come to dominate many sporting cultures because it is simple and it is flexible.

Football's simplicity means that pretty much anyone can pick up a ball, put down a couple of markers for a goal and start playing some sort of game. Everyone has a basic understanding of most of the rules and so a match can break out almost anywhere.

In terms of flexibility, shirt numbers offer an interesting angle. In some comparable team sports, the number on your shirt tends to give the audience an idea of a player's sphere of influence. In football, with the exception of the number 1 shirt (and even that is by convention rather than law: a goalie could play in any number they negotiated with their club if they wanted), shirt numbers don't really mean anything.

Yes, lower numbers tend to be more defensively minded and most players with stars in their eyes are looking at the number 10 shirt, but broadly speaking, outfield players can end up anywhere during any particular phase of play. This is why you have defenders making runs from their own boxes while midfielders drop back to provide cover, and why tactics in football are often built around the capabilities of individual team members rather than the functions of a specific role.

It means that the game is constantly and quickly innovating in a way that other sports struggle to achieve.

It is basically the sort of thing that folk who really get football understand and can follow but goes way over the heads of anyone who doesn't have that depth of knowledge. It's also why throwing money at a football team doesn't always get you to the top of the Premier League.

·A LITTLE BOOK OF FOOTBALL·

★ GEORGE BEST ★

Best joined Manchester United in 1963, just at the point when British society was moving into the swinging sixties and a short back and sides was starting to be seen as really square, daddy-o. Or something equally ungroovy. George Best epitomised the move from suits, Brylcreem and quiffs to the shaggy, 'anything goes' style of the late 1960s.

Social commentary and cheap shots about haircuts aside, George Best was, by all accounts, a phenomenal football player. He was one of the new generation of players who, despite the heavy clod of British pitches at the time, could move the ball with the grace and elegance that modern footballers can only achieve on a perfectly manicured modern Premier League pitch. He mesmerised the people in the stands and the growing number of people watching on TV. As well as opposition defences.

He played for Manchester United 361 times in the league, finding the back of the net 137 times over 11 glorious years as part of a trinity within the team comprising Best, Bobby Charlton and Denis Law. Together, they won England's top flight twice (it would have been three times but the noisy neighbours snatched the league away from them by two points in 1967/68), the Charity Shield twice and the European Cup once.

Best also played 37 times for Northern Ireland, scoring nine goals. It should probably have been 10: during a game against England, Gordon Banks was about to kick the ball downfield but, in the split second after tossing the ball in the air to kick it, Best got a kick in first, which lobbed the ball over the goalie and enabled him to sprint past Banks and head the ball into the goal. The goal was disallowed, though, because Best's foot was perceived to be high.

Once he moved on from United, he played for various teams around the world without ever settling on a new home, his skills gradually deteriorating as off-field distractions took their toll. Despite this, Old Trafford, and the rest of the world, will always celebrate what he achieved with the ball at his feet and the style that he achieved it with.

'Maradona good, Pelé better, George Best', as they used to say.

· A LITTLE BOOK OF FOOTBALL ·

"The person that said winning isn't everything, never won anything."

US football player Mia Hamm.

· A LITTLE BOOK OF FOOTBALL ·

★ WILD GOAT CHASE ★

The Greatest of All Time (GOAT) debate rages across social media, with opinions differing according to team allegiance and your footballing era (granted, there are relatively few septuagenarians that are particularly active on social media, so the debate tends to be skewed towards modern players, but you get the point).

Let's get the first point over with ... There is really only one contender for the title of GOAT that has come through the British system, but in a lot of ways George Best's career didn't have the consistency that marks out a GOAT from an exceptional talent.

The reality is that there are probably four players that have a decent shout at being known as the GOAT: Diego Maradona, Lionel Messi, Edson Arantes do Nascimento (Pelé to his friends and admirers) and Cristiano Ronaldo. If you sat down with your opera-loving aunt and your *Star Trek*-devoted cousin, those are the four footballers that even they would have a decent shout at naming.

It's fascinating that Ronaldo and Messi have both emerged over the last 20 years. Pretty much every aspect of football has changed over the last 50 years — from the equipment used and the pitches that the players roam, right the way through to the physical and emotional support that professionals receive. The money's a little better as well. These factors could have played into two phenomenal talents emerging in the same era, although it could be just coincidence and it could be that we have simply been spoilt.

The goal's a goal

Perhaps the simplest gauge of a player's prowess and their right to be held above all others is how often they find the net, but even here it's complicated.

Taking into account recorded games since he became a professional, Maradona, scored 293 goals in 581 games. Dividing one by the other offers a goal to game percentage of 50.4%, which is low in comparison with Messi, who has made 819 appearances and provided 630 goals, giving 76.9% and Ronaldo, who has played 927 games and found the net 680 times, which makes 73.3%.

Back in Pelé's day, meanwhile, stats weren't recorded quite as obsessively as they are today, but he is thought to have scored 683 goals over 739 appearances for club and country, giving him a terrifying goal to game percentage of 92.4%.

Messi and Ronaldo are both still playing, but it's going to take some fairly impressive goal gluts to bring them anywhere near Pelé's totals. But here's where the comparisons become irrelevant: can you compare the Brazil team of the 1950s and 1960s, which was absolutely dripping with talent across the pitch, with the more recent Argentinian and Portuguese teams, which have only been very good? At the same time, can you compare Pelé's Santos with the more recent teams in the English, Italian or Spanish leagues, which also tend to have world-class talent in every position?

You could compare numbers of trophies and disciplinary records, but that's just stats. You can argue about whether the greatest players in the history of the game are those lower down the pitch but, in the end, with apologies to drummers and bass players, most people only remember the singers and the lead guitarists.

Trying to work out who is the greatest football player of all time is a bit of a thankless task, really. There have been so many phenomenal players that have graced the football pitch that it is difficult to pick one, and the reality is that the players that emerge to join the legendary pantheon are only ever playing the opponents of their time and using the equipment of the era. What could Pelé have achieved with a pair of modern boots? Equally, would anyone have heard of Ronaldo if he was trying to ply his trade in a pair of heavy leather steel-capped work boots? Could Messi have coped with the heavy mud of a 1950s football pitch, and would anyone remember the name Maradona if there had been VAR in 1984?

One final thought. Taking the opinions of ten relatively reputable sites and their analysis of the best four players in the history of football, you can see a fair amount of consistency.

Source	Beckenbauer	Cruyff	Maradona	Messi	Pelé	Ronaldo
FourFourTwo Magazine	x	x	3	1	2	4
Givemesport.com	x	x	4	1	3	2
90min.com	4	x	2	1	3	x
Sportbible.com	x	4	3	1	2	x
The Mirror (using Chat GPT)	x	x	2	3	1	4
Daily Mail	x	4	3	1	2	x
bbc.co.uk	x	x	4	2	1	3
Soccergoatss.com	x	x	3	2	1	4
The Sun	x	x	2	1	4	3
Radio Times	x	x	2	1	4	3

Applying expert levels of analysis, the likes of which have not been seen since the last school sports day (writing this information on the back of a beer mat) and applying a complex algorithm developed specially for this book (we assigned four points for first, three points for second two points for third and one point for fourth and then added them up on our fingers and toes) gives us these exclusive numbers:

Player	Sum of Score
Messi	36
Pelé	27
Maradona	22
Ronaldo	12
Cruyff	2
Beckenbauer	1
Grand Total	100

Does it tell us anything new?
Not really.